# New Knowledge
## *for*
# New Results

A Comprehensive Strategy for Reducing
Skyrocketing Medical Costs

## Robert E. Herron, Ph.D., MBA

1st WORLD
PUBLISHING

# New Knowledge for New Results

## Robert E. Herron, Ph.D., MBA

© Robert E. Herron 2008

Published by 1stWorld Publishing
1100 North 4th St., Fairfield, Iowa 52556
tel: 641-209-5000 • fax: 641-209-3001
web: www.1stworldpublishing.com

First Edition

LCCN: 2007942941

SoftCover 978-1-4218-9843-8

HardCover 978-1-4218-9842-1

eBook ISBN: 978-1-4218-9844-5

This book is dedicated in loving memory to my father

Colonel Robert M. Herron III
United States Military Academy Class of 1945

March 11, 1922 – April 16, 2006

and to my sister

Frances Anne Herron

April 15, 1954 – September 24, 2004

# Acknowledgements

I am deeply indebted to numerous people who have helped me create this book. Foremost among these great people is my loving wife, Ginette, who has helped me in countless, invaluable ways that made completion of this work possible. I would also like to acknowledge my father, Col. Robert M. Herron III, and mother, Sophie Z. Herron, and many others who have also provided generous support and inspiration over the many years of research that was needed for writing this book.

Heather Jones has given comprehensive editorial assistance and excellent advice in revising this book. She has exceptional talents and is a genius with words. Her incredible ability to help shape rough drafts into clear prose would be a valuable asset in any writing project.

Michael Warner also contributed editorial assistance in amending this manuscript. Michael possesses a penetrating insight into reality and a special gift for giving life to scientific facts. Special appreciation goes to the late Charles N. Alexander, Ph.D. who first suggested that I write this book. My deepest appreciation goes to His Holiness Maharishi Mahesh Yogi who provided many important insights and profound knowledge on how health care systems should work.

# Table of Contents

Introduction . . . . . . . . . . . . . . . . . . . . . . . . . . . . . . . . . . . . . . . . 17

## The Problems with Medical Systems

Chapter 1
Does Spending More for Medical Care Ensure Better Health? . . . . . . . . . 27

Chapter 2
Amend the Medical Theory to Save the Health System. . . . . . . . . . . . . . 45

## Innovative Solutions

Chapter 3
Health and the New Medical Model . . . . . . . . . . . . . . . . . . . . . . . . . . . . 69

Chapter 4
Something Old, Something New: The Value of
Scientifically Verified Complementary and Alternative
Medicine (CAM). . . . . . . . . . . . . . . . . . . . . . . . . . . . . . . . . . . . . . . . . . 77

Chapter 5
An Example of a CAM Method That Decreases
Medical Costs . . . . . . . . . . . . . . . . . . . . . . . . . . . . . . . . . . . . . . . . . . . . 95

# Much Needed Solutions

Chapter 6

An Ounce of Prevention...Tons of Savings for Society. . . . . . . . . . . . . . 115

Chapter 7

Improve and Expand Primary Care. . . . . . . . . . . . . . . . . . . . . . . . . . . . . 131

Chapter 8

An Overlooked Opportunity for Cutting Medical Expenses . . . . . . . . . 147

# Summary and Actions Steps

Chapter 9

Suggestions to Reduce Medical Expenses and Improve Health . . . . . . . . 161

Chapter 10

The Health Care System Transformation . . . . . . . . . . . . . . . . . . . . . . . 183

Appendix I. . . . . . . . . . . . . . . . . . . . . . . . . . . . . . . . . . . . . . . . . . . . . . . . 187

Appendix II . . . . . . . . . . . . . . . . . . . . . . . . . . . . . . . . . . . . . . . . . . . . . . . 191

References . . . . . . . . . . . . . . . . . . . . . . . . . . . . . . . . . . . . . . . . . . . . . . . . 193

# Figures and Tables

Introduction

0.1 Estimated Annual Medical Expenses Due to
   Unhealthy Lifestyle Factors that Contribute to
   Chronic Conditions in the United States of America . . . . . . . . . . . . 21

Chapter 1

1.1 Medical Expenses Have Been Rising Worldwide for
   Many Years: Total Expenditures on Health per Person
   from 1990 to 2004 . . . . . . . . . . . . . . . . . . . . . . . . . . . . . . . . . . . . . . 28

1.2 As the Funding for Medical Services Increases, Money
   for Other Important Priorities Decreases. . . . . . . . . . . . . . . . . . . . . 31

1.3 OECD Infant Mortality: Deaths per 1,000 Live
   Births, 2004 . . . . . . . . . . . . . . . . . . . . . . . . . . . . . . . . . . . . . . . . . . . . 34

1.4 Females: Average Years of Healthy Life Expectancy at
   Birth, 2002 . . . . . . . . . . . . . . . . . . . . . . . . . . . . . . . . . . . . . . . . . . . . . 35

1.5 Males: Average Years of Healthy Life Expectancy at
   Birth, 2002 . . . . . . . . . . . . . . . . . . . . . . . . . . . . . . . . . . . . . . . . . . . . . 36

1.6 Relationship of 2004 Total per Capita Expenditure on
   Health and Infant Deaths per 1,000 Live Births:
   Comparing Life Expectancy at Birth and Percent of
   GNP Spent on Medical Services . . . . . . . . . . . . . . . . . . . . . . . . . . . . 37

1.7 Life Expectancy at Birth, 1900–2000 . . . . . . . . . . . . . . . . . . . . . . . 39

1.8 Percent of GNP Spent on Medical Care, 1900–2000 . . . . . . . . . . . . 39

1.9 Infant Mortality Rate and GNP Spent on Medical
   Care, 1900–2000 . . . . . . . . . . . . . . . . . . . . . . . . . . . . . . . . . . . . . . . . 41

1.10 Total Death Rate and GNP Spent on Medical Care,
   1900–2000 . . . . . . . . . . . . . . . . . . . . . . . . . . . . . . . . . . . . . . . . . . . . . 42

Chapter 2

2.1 Knowledge is the Basis of Action. . . . . . . . . . . . . . . . . . . . . . . . . . . 45

2.2 Most Fundamental General System. . . . . . . . . . . . . . . . . . . . . . . . 48

2.3 Comprehensive General Systems Overview of the
Medical Sector. . . . . . . . . . . . . . . . . . . . . . . . . . . . . . . . . . . . . . . . . . 49

2.4 Biomedical Model of Causality: The Doctrine of
Specific Etiology . . . . . . . . . . . . . . . . . . . . . . . . . . . . . . . . . . . . . . . . 53

2.5 The Reductionist Strategy for Obtaining Knowledge . . . . . . . . . . . . 56

2.6 An Aid in the Acquisition of Complete Knowledge . . . . . . . . . . . . . 57

Chapter 3

3.1 New Global Integration of Medical Models . . . . . . . . . . . . . . . . . . . 70

3.2 The Old and Emerging Knowledge
Subsystems Compared . . . . . . . . . . . . . . . . . . . . . . . . . . . . . . . . . . . 72

Chapter 4

4.1 U.S. Visits to CAM Practitioners Surpass Visits to
Primary Care Physicians . . . . . . . . . . . . . . . . . . . . . . . . . . . . . . . . . . 78

4.2 Most Conventional and CAM Methods Have Not
Been Tested for Effectiveness and Safety . . . . . . . . . . . . . . . . . . . . . . 81

4.3 Annual Total Medical Expenditures With and
Without Chiropractic Care . . . . . . . . . . . . . . . . . . . . . . . . . . . . . . . . 88

4.4 Average Hospitalizations for Back Pain Patients With
and Without Chiropractic Care. . . . . . . . . . . . . . . . . . . . . . . . . . . . . 88

4.5 The Cost-effectiveness of Treating Migraine
Headaches: Comparison of the Costs per QALY
Gained for Acupuncture and Usual Care Drug . . . . . . . . . . . . . . . . . 91

# Chapter 5

5.1 Estimated Effect of Selected Health Risk Factors on Annual Medical Costs ........................................ 96

5.2 Possible Paths for Chronic Stress to Contribute to High Medical Expenses ........................................ 98

5.3 Comparison of the Effectiveness of Relaxation Procedures in Reducing Trait Anxiety ........................ 103

5.4 Comparison of the Effectiveness of Methods for Reducing Cigarette Use ........................................ 103

5.5 The TM Technique Reduced Medical Expenses of People Over Age 65 ........................................ 107

5.6 TM Subjects Had Reduced Medical Payments Each Year for Six Years ........................................ 108

5.7 The TM Technique Reduced the Payments to Physicians for Treating Consistent High-Cost People ........ 109

# Chapter 6

6.1 Why Not Fund Fully That Which Has the Greatest Potential to Improve Health? ........................ 116

6.2 Comparison of Infant Death Rates in Cuba and the United States ........................................ 117

6.3 Average Years of Healthy Life Expectancy at Birth (HALE) and Per Capita Expenditure on Health ........ 118

6.4 Spending on Different Types of Medical Care in the U.S.A. ........................................ 121

6.5 Neglected: Actual Causes of Costly Death, Disease, and Injury ........................................ 123

6.6 Preventing Type 2 Diabetes in Adults with Impaired Glucose Tolerance: A Comparison of Lifestyle Modification versus Metformin ........................................ 125

6.7 Net Amount of Medical Costs Saved by Removing Lead from Older U.S. Homes ........................ 127

Chapter 7

7.1 Income Comparison between Primary Care
Physicians and Specialists . . . . . . . . . . . . . . . . . . . . . . . . . . . . . . . . . . 132

7.2 The Roles of the Primary Care Physician . . . . . . . . . . . . . . . . . . . . . 133

7.3 In U.S. Population, on Average, Primary Care Saves Lives:
All Cause Mortality Comparison between Specialty Care
and Family Medicine Primary Care . . . . . . . . . . . . . . . . . . . . . . . . . . 137

7.4 Increased Spending on Primary Care Reduced
Total Medical Expenses . . . . . . . . . . . . . . . . . . . . . . . . . . . . . . . . . . . . 141

7.5 Estimated Percentages of Annual Usage of Types
of Medical Services in U. S. . . . . . . . . . . . . . . . . . . . . . . . . . . . . . . . . 143

Chapter 8

8.1 Percentage of Annual Total Medical Expenses Incurred
by Highest-Cost 10% of People in United States . . . . . . . . . . . . . . 148

8.2 Percentage of Annual Total Medical Expenses Incurred
by Highest-Cost 1% of People in United States . . . . . . . . . . . . . . . . 150

8.3 Percentage of Annual Total Medical Expenses Incurred
by Highest-Cost 5% of People in United States . . . . . . . . . . . . . . . . 151

Chapter 9

9.1 Proposed New Structure for Medical Systems:
Re-organizing Priorities for Funding, Research,
and Prestige in Medical Systems . . . . . . . . . . . . . . . . . . . . . . . . . . . . . 163

# Introduction

*"Without health, there is no happiness. An attention to health, then, should take the place of every other object."*

—Thomas Jefferson, Third President of the United States of America and author of the American Declaration of Independence[1]

Why is it that most nations spend so much to care for the sick, but so little to prevent disease and ensure health? Why are our medical efforts so misdirected and costly? Incomplete medical knowledge could be a factor. Let's begin our search for solutions by looking at how medical systems affect real people.

While writing this book, I traveled often to the University of Iowa libraries in Iowa City to do research. On one visit, I stopped at a convenience store to buy a drink. In Iowa City, mainly young university students work at these stores. However, on this day at the cash register there was a lady in her mid-thirties. As I purchased my beverage, I told her about my writing project. She said that she would find my book very interesting, and then told me her story.

This lady had a secure and comfortable life in the past, but found herself widowed and without health insurance. She had a child with an incurable illness, and her little boy required several expensive medical treatments each month to stay alive. Her son also needed costly medications. Even with some charity and government money helping her, she had to pay huge medical bills every month, or her child would die. To pay these high expenses, she worked at three minimum wage jobs, two of which were full time at convenience stores. She worked her three jobs for long days, usually seven days a week. This schedule gave her little time to care for her ailing son. She lived a grim life of strain and sleep deprivation. However, she told her story without complaint, self-pity, or emotion. She exuded a gentle, balanced determination. From her eyes shone a light of transcendent dignity and character that few have. If you appreciate heroic virtue, she was one of God's angels. Nevertheless, she had become a virtual slave of the medical system. Her whole life revolved around paying medical bills to keep her son alive. As I departed to continue my journey, I wondered how long her health would last with such a demanding work regimen and insufficient rest. How long would her son survive with so little care from his loving, but over-worked mother? In addition, I wondered how many other people without health insurance or who were underinsured had also become slaves of their medical bills in the United States. A study published in the *Journal of the American Medical Association* found that in 2003 nearly 49 million Americans spent more than 10% of their families' income on medical care. Of these, almost 19 million were spending more than 20% of family income on medical treatment.[2] In the U.S., medical expenses are a major source of credit card debt and personal bankruptcy. This burden falls disproportionately on those least able to pay.[3] According to the World Health Organization, rising medical expenses push millions of people into poverty each year across the planet. In addition, researchers have also estimated that America's failure to provide medical insurance coverage for its entire population has contributed to at least 18,000 deaths annually.[4] As I drove away, I vowed to write this book for these people.

We could think of this courageous lady as a micro-example or metaphor for the numerous countries that run on an endless, increasingly painful treadmill to pay higher and higher medical expenses each year, with little measurable improvement in national health. Like the brave lady in Iowa City, each day is a battle for survival for many nations. The economic strain of rising costs is tearing apart the social fabric of families, provinces, and countries. Even the wealthiest nation on Earth, the United States of America, has a medical cost crisis dragging down its economy and demoralizing its citizens. Modern medicine seems to be on a collision course with economic reality worldwide. Something has to change. In the end, because of the interconnectedness of the global economy, we all pay for these skyrocketing medical expenditures indirectly or directly.

> This book contains major innovations. In contrast with previous general systems evaluations, we will examine the body of knowledge that informs and guides almost every aspect of the medical system.

Most nations have tried to improve their health and reduce medical expenditures with superficial strategies that failed to address the underlying causes of their problems. We will offer comprehensive remedies for these root causes.

We will explore the effectiveness of modern medicine from a perspective called general systems, which is a discipline that attempts to evaluate organizations from a holistic, interdisciplinary viewpoint. It applies a comprehensive integration of both analysis and synthesis. The goal of the general systems approach is to make holistic improvements. In medicine, this strategy has been applied many times in the past. In contrast with previous general systems evaluations, we will examine the body of knowledge that informs and guides almost every aspect of the medical system.

We assume that modern medicine has more scientific validity and credibility than it actually has. In any system, knowledge is the basis of action and results. Accurate and complete knowledge is needed to produce the desired outcomes, especially in health care systems. The failure of medical theory is the inability of systematic knowledge to describe and explain phenomena accurately, reliably, and comprehensively. There is an emerging body of research and clinical experience suggesting that the "knowledge" that guides modern medicine may be incomplete and inaccurate in several important areas. Because faulty information drives the system, the failure of medical theory appears to be the hidden cause of most problems within health care systems, including soaring expenses and variable effectiveness.

> Because knowledge drives the system, the failure of medical theory is the hidden source of most problems within health care systems, including soaring expenses, excessive mistakes, negative drug side effects, and variable effectiveness.

When we hear the term "modern" medicine we assume this means that our health care system is based on the most advanced science available. Today, however, the dominant understanding of how health is produced is still the "machine model" of medicine, which is based mainly on seventeenth-century science. The machine model tends to divert funding toward expensive and risky high-technology treatments and away from cost-effective preventive approaches.

New discoveries have dramatically altered the knowledge that enables us to understand nature and health. Medicine has neglected incorporating most of these important changes for many years. Knowledge is the most crucial component of any system because it has the power to guide or misguide the entire system.

If incomplete or incorrect fundamental knowledge misguides medical professionals, this flaw can cause entire systems to operate poorly, in spite of the best efforts of the sincere and competent people within the system. If we find that there are better

> **Knowledge is the most crucial component of any system because it has the power to guide or misguide the entire system.**

options than continuing with the medical *status quo*, we must be prepared to change the health care system. Sickness is the basis of high medical expenses. As we improve the health of a nation, corporation, or family, high medical expenses will decline as the number of sick people greatly diminishes. Prominent health researcher Kenneth Thorpe has explained:

> Approximately 63 percent of the rise in real per capita spending is traced to a rise in treated disease prevalence. This rise is caused by rising prevalence of disease in the population, changing clinical thresholds for diagnosing and treating disease, and innovations (new technology) in treatment.[5]

In recent years worldwide, there have been increases in what are called chronic illnesses, diseases, or disorders. Chronic diseases are those ailments that last for long periods or reoccur often. Diabetes, asthma, peptic ulcers, arthritis, Parkinson's disease, multiple sclerosis, high blood pressure, and cardiovascular disorders are examples of chronic disorders. Once acquired, these diseases tend to persist indefinitely and are distinguished from acute illnesses, which are ailments with a short duration. Most of these chronic ailments could have been prevented.

In this book, the main focus is on preventing both the physical and mental need for medical treatment. As the use of medical care decreases steeply, the prices for medical goods and services will also decline. The majority of medical expenditures are caused by very sick people who need extensive hospital and specialist care. Most of these costs are incurred each year only by a small percentage of the population. Typically, these highest-cost patients have numerous chronic diseases for which modern medicine has no cure, but only symptomatic relief. In the United States, chronic disorders account for 75% to 80% of national medical expenditures. This trend occurs in most nations. Why are chronic conditions incurable? To find the answer, we need to re-examine our most basic assumptions on how to produce health. We need to re-evaluate the completeness and accuracy of the entire structure of knowledge that guides most medical activities and funding. We need to know more on how the medical system really works and how to transform it.

**0.1 Estimated Annual Medical Expenses Due to Unhealthy Lifestyle Factors that Contribute to Chronic Conditions in the United States of America**

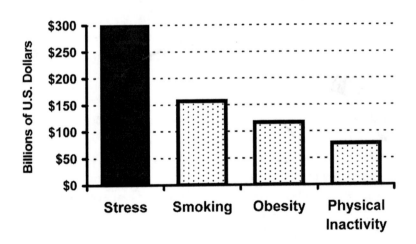

Data Sources: U.S. Dept. of Health and Human Services: *Healthy People 2010: Understanding and Improving Health,* Washington, DC: Government Printing Office, 2000. Center for Disease Control and Prevention, *An Ounce of Prevention....What are the Returns?* 2nd edition, Atlanta, GA: Dept. of Health and Human Services, 1999. *Healthy People 2000: National Health Promotion and Disease Prevention Objectives,* Washington, DC: Government Printing Office, 1990.

As Dr. W. Edwards Deming has explained, "Every system is perfectly designed to achieve the results it gets." If Deming is right, then our medical systems are "perfectly designed" to produce high expenditures, variable quality, numerous medical errors, negative medication side effects, an epidemic of chronic diseases, and many other problems. This situation seems true for most countries. How can we change the system to increase effectiveness and decrease costs?

In spite of great reform attempts, major problems persist and even increase in medical systems worldwide. In the United States, medical insurance premiums have been increasing faster than the growth of the average income, gross national product, and inflation rates. This situation is unsustainable. The urgency of the problem is something upon which most people agree, regardless of their political viewpoint.

For instance, in the United States, as the former Republican Secretary of Health and Human Services Tommy Thompson has explained: "The health system is so stretched and stressed that something has to be done. The health care system is in dire need of some sort of transformation."[6] Former Democratic Vice President Al Gore observed: "Our current system is quite literally collapsing."[6] The Republican Governor of California Arnold Schwarzenegger stated: "The spiraling cost of health care is nearing the breaking point—not just in California but across the nation.... We must find ways to lower the cost of health care. We cannot continue as we have."[7]

In the United States, many proposals have been suggested to improve the medical system. Often health care reform has been discussed in financial terms, such as adjusting monetary incentives to encourage employees to use medical services judiciously, enhancing market competition, increasing tax deductions for medical services, and creating health savings accounts. These are partial and superficial solutions that will provide little improvement to national health and reduction of total medical expenditures. In this book, we will see that the medical systems of the world need complete re-structuring. As Ezekiel J. Emanuel and Victor R. Fuchs have explained:

> This profusion of proposals means that health care is getting more attention, and this makes reform more likely. But these proposals are like band-aids and fall far short of what our sick health-care system

needs.... By building on the existing health-care system, these reform proposals entrench the perverse incentives.[8]

While the urgency of the problem is generally recognized, comprehensive solutions are sparse.

If we look at the big picture of world events and human history, we see there is only one constant: Everything changes eventually. All aspects of life are constantly developing and evolving into something more advanced than in the past. Sometimes, unfortunately, systems also seem to slide backwards. This book will help provide knowledge that will stimulate discussion and consideration of a wider range of possibilities than previously considered for improving the medical systems of the world.

We will focus mainly on the medical system of the United States of America because (1) U.S. advanced medical technology is believed to be the best in the world, (2) its medical system is thought to be an ideal that other nations should follow, if they want to have a modern high-technology health care system, and (3) there are more data readily available in the United States than most other nations. In this book, however, we will present solutions that could be applied successfully worldwide. The most important point is to expand and improve disease prevention and health promotion. For an efficient and cost-effective health care system, *what we spend on* is more important than how much we spend, or how we finance and deliver medical treatment.

The strategies that are suggested avoid diminishing people's choices or attempting to reduce medical expenses through unethical methods, such as denying or restricting medical care to those who really need it. Rather, this book will show how we can use more comprehensive knowledge to redirect our medical spending to best improve health at the lowest expense.

> This book will present scientific research to show how we can use more comprehensive knowledge to redirect our medical spending to best improve health at the lowest expense.

# The Problems with Medical Systems

In Chapter 1, we will examine the growth of medical expenses and determine what value the United States is getting for its huge investment.

In Chapter 2, we will examine the validity of the body of knowledge that informs and guides almost every aspect of the medical system.

# Chapter 1

# Does Spending More for Medical Care Ensure Better Health?

*"The modern world, despite a surfeit of obfuscation, complication, and downright deceit, is not impenetrable, is not unknowable, and —if the right questions are asked—is even more intriguing than we think. All it takes is a new way of looking."*

—Steven D. Levitt, Ph.D. and Stephen J. Dubner[1]

In this chapter, we will explore a "new way of looking" at the expenditures that the United States and other nations pay for medical services by connecting those costs with the health results of the medical system. An analogy may help us grasp the big, complex picture. Despite the constant publicity on new medical miracles, modern medicine is actually like an aging car. Have you, or a friend, ever owned an old car that performed inconsistently? The aged machine was chronically inefficient and costly. Perhaps it burned oil and had a top speed of 30 mph when it worked at all. To keep the old clunker going, you paid larger and larger auto repair bills with no end in sight. After adding up how much you spent, did you eventually realize that the monthly payments or rental fees for a new vehicle would have been less costly than supporting the old wreck? Beneath the shining veneer of advanced science, modern medicine may be like an old car with ever-increasing expenses and less than optimal performance.

Life and health are infinitely more important than money. Nevertheless, financial considerations strongly influence much decision making worldwide. An adequate level of medical spending appears to be necessary to maintain the health of a nation. However, the consequences of unduly high and rapidly increasing medical care expenses and failure to cure or prevent chronic diseases have far-reaching negative effects on society. Many of these consequences have been unexpected, unrecognized, and ignored in the past. We will mention only a few because the global press and other writers and researchers have begun to explore these problems extensively. The main focus of this book is solutions, not problems. We need new ways of looking at the effectiveness of the health care systems of the world.

First, we will look at total per person expenditures on health, which are the average of all expenses incurred for medical services for individual citizens within a nation annually.

**1.1 Medical Expenses Have Been Rising Worldwide for Many Years: Total Expenditures on Health per Person from 1990 to 2004**

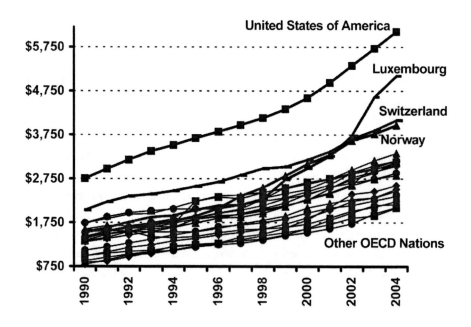

Data Source: Organisation for Economic Cooperation and Development (OECD) Health Data, 2006.

ROBERT E. HERRON

The main point of the previous chart is that every nation shown and almost all other countries globally (not shown) have rising medical expenditures, which usually cause many serious problems. The United States has the highest medical expenditures in the world. Yet, the trend for only one nation is not our primary interest. Our concern is for the total picture worldwide. The most salient observation is that health care expenses are rising for virtually all nations despite numerous attempts to control these costs. We might consider why.

Most global economic trends tend to be cyclical, periodically rising and declining over time. In contrast, we observe that medical expenditures exhibit a non-cyclical trend. They consistently keep getting higher worldwide regardless of other economic improvements or changes. Cost containment strategies sometimes provide relief by temporarily slowing the rates of increase in medical expenses. However, neither governmental regulatory policies nor the "free market" consumer-driven strategies have slowed the growth of medical spending in the long term. Thus far, no cost reduction or containment program has succeeded for a long period. These plans inevitably fail because they fail to address the underlying causes of the high medical cost problems. If remedial action is delayed, many countries might find themselves in a situation similar to that of the United States, with very high costs that negatively affect their economies.

Almost all nations have different systems of financing and delivering medical care to their people. Nevertheless, no country has an ideal medical system. Some are socialist, while others are capitalist.

> The fact that most nations have rising medical expenses regardless of their widely different ways of financing and delivering medical care suggests there is a deeper, underlying cause of these costs.

Some countries have single payers, and others have multiple payers for medical treatment. Each nation delivers care in widely different ways. Yet, they all have problems with increasing medical expenditures. This observation is important because many policy leaders and health economists attribute their medical systems' costs mainly to financing and delivering problems. The fact that most nations have rising medical expenses regardless of these highly diverse arrangements may suggest that there is a deeper, underlying cause of these costs that is unrelated to the financing of medical treatment or economic system.

The medical expenditures of most nations have been generally increasing since the end of World War II. We might wonder what impact this spending has on individual lives and the rest of a country's economy. In other words, why does unduly high medical spending matter?

## What Do We Give Up When We Spend More on Medicine?

Misdirected and excessive spending hurts everyone. To understand fully, we must put rising medical expenses into a bigger perspective than only the health sector, even though it is the largest industry in most wealthy nations. Let us look at the world as economists see life's transactions. Whenever a person chooses to spend a dollar or any other monetary unit on something, they gain that product. This individual is, however, also giving up the opportunity to spend that dollar on some other product or service. Economists call the options eliminated by making a spending decision the *opportunity costs* of that particular investment choice. In other words, what do we give up when we choose to spend increasing amounts on medical care?

As increasing percentages of a nation's income are spent for medical treatment, there are correspondingly lower percentages of funding available for other important priorities, such as improving a country's standard of living, educational systems, energy supply, poverty reduction, infrastructure, national defense, and other pressing needs. Most of these tradeoffs have been made without any input, approval, or vote from the general population who will suffer the most from excessive medical spending. As the proportion of medical expenses increases, governments will be less effective in fulfilling their parental role of caring for their people.

For instance, job creation is an increasingly crucial issue for almost all nations. As progressively more funding goes into the medical industry, less investment money is available to help other industries create innovative products and new jobs. This is frequently true even when the general economy is improving. In addition, when employers pay a major percentage of their employees' medical expenses, the cost of maintaining current employees' health benefits can become so high that creating new jobs becomes difficult, and too frequently impossible. In fact, many companies in the U.S. have had to lay off workers to keep their health insurance plan viable for their remaining employees.

**1.2 As the Funding for Medical Services Increases, Money for Other Important Priorities Decreases**

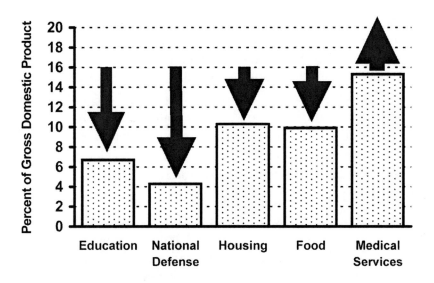

Total annual percent of U.S. GDP spent for selected areas from all sources public & private

Data Sources: OECD, 2005, Bureau for Economic Analysis, 2004, Centers for Medicare & Medicaid Services, 2005

Let's consider hidden income loses. Often without knowing it, employees have given up significant amounts of income for medical care either directly or indirectly. For instance, the employers have not been able to give the pay increases that their workers deserved for increased productivity because they spent the firm's increased revenues to cover skyrocketing medical expenses. This hidden loss of income undermines the quality of life of the individual and family. Since consumer spending drives most economic activity, the diversion of increasing amounts into medical care will also weaken most national economies in the long term.

Furthermore, increased percentages of GDP going into the health sector have created millions of unproductive medical jobs. Unproductive jobs are defined as employment that consumes more resources than the benefits it creates for a nation in the long term. These new jobs give the appearance of economic growth because the national output of services has increased. Soaring employment in the medical sector has been welcomed as a way of counterbalancing the millions of jobs that have been lost through the outsourcing of work to countries with low labor costs. Yet, in the long term, unproductive job creation is net loss, not a gain. This is especially troubling in light of a report from Boston University School of Public Health stating that soaring medical expenditures absorbed 25% of U.S. economic growth from 2000 to 2005.[2] The total effects of this ballooning employment are often undetected because the productivity, quality, and actual impact of medical services on health are so difficult to measure.

An example of unproductive job creation is the more than $300 billion spent annually in the United States for the administration of the non-government portion of the medical system in 2003. The United States has the highest medical administrative expenses in the world.[3-6] This huge paper-processing network employs thousands of people mainly in the private, for-profit sector. Most of these jobs are almost totally unproductive.[3-6] There is no scientific evidence showing that this massive paper shuffling improves the health of a nation.

As we expand our view to consider global spending, we might wonder how the excessive diversion of funds into national health sectors affects the entire planet. For example, as more is spent on medical care globally, less is spent to discover and develop new scientific and technological breakthroughs in other areas that are also important. Are we willing to give up future scientific discoveries and inventions that may have a greater impact worldwide than electricity, computers, or airplanes in return for unnecessarily costly medical treatments? We all need to re-examine how much we are willing to sacrifice for the medical *status quo*.

## Medical Spending Reality Check

Major reports have compared international health system outcomes. In 2000, the World Health Organization (WHO) published a report titled The World Health Report 2000, Health Systems: Improving Performance. This report compared the performance of the medical systems of 191 countries. In this evaluation, the WHO found the United States spent the most for medical care, but ranked surprising low for important measures of medical system effectiveness:[7]

- 24th for disability-adjusted life expectancy (life expectancy minus years of disability);
- 37th on overall medical system performance;
- 72nd for efficiency in improving citizens' general health.

Basically, the WHO found that the citizens of the United States, on average, had close to the worst health for a developed nation. Americans also had one of the world's least fair, or equitable, ways of financing and delivering medical treatment.[7] On the WHO measure of fairness of medical financing, the United States ranked 54th.[7]

In 2007, the U.S. Census Bureau's web site posted an international comparison of 222 nations for several health measures. The United States of America was ranked 42nd for life expectancy at birth. Today, on average, U.S. citizens are living longer than ever before. However, other countries have made much greater progress in improving disease prevention, health promotion, universal medical insurance, economic equity, and other factors that improve population health than the U.S. Let's look at another way of measuring medical system effectiveness.

We will examine infant mortality rates, which are thought to be a very comprehensive indicator of overall medical system performance. The reason is that to achieve low infant death rates, many tasks have to be done correctly throughout a medical system. The following chart presents data from the Organisation for Economic Co-operation and Development (OECD). The OECD is a group of 30 nations that work together to strengthen democracy and market economies within their countries and worldwide. Most of the OECD nations are highly developed with advanced high-technology medical systems. This chart for 2004 shows 28 OECD nations' infant deaths per 1,000 live births. Japan and Iceland had the lowest infant death rates. The U.S. had the highest infant mortality rate among these countries despite its superior medical technology and greatest medical spending.

**1.3 OECD Infant Mortality: Deaths per 1,000 Live Births, 2004**

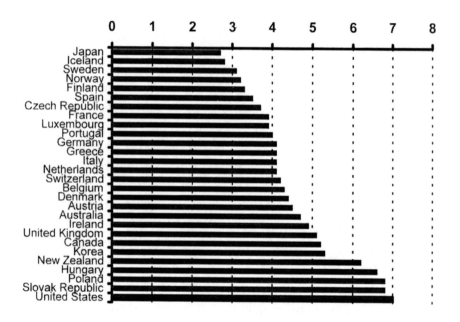

Data Source: Organisation for Economic Co-operation and Development Health Data, 2006

Let's look at another relatively comprehensive measure of medical system performance. Healthy Life Expectancy at birth (HALE)[8] is considered a more comprehensive measure of medical system performance than other general indicators, such as crude Life Expectancy, which is based on death rates, not health.[9] HALE shows how long, on average, people within a country live in good health. With HALE, the years spent in poor health and disability are subtracted from the usual Life Expectancy data.[9] The World Health Organization has defined Healthy

ROBERT E. HERRON

Life Expectancy at birth as the "average number of years that a person can expect to live in full health by taking into account years lived in less than full health due to disease and/or injury."[10] A population's living longer in serious diseased states or with disabilities indicates that a medical system has failed to achieve its primary mission of enhancing the nation's health. In contrast, when a country's citizens are living longer without disease this suggests that a medical system is effective.

In the following charts for men and women, we see the average years of Healthy Life Expectancy at birth for the top performing 29 countries in 2002. Japan (77.7 years for females and 72.3 years for males) has the longest life span in good health while the United States (71.3 years for females and 67.2 years for males) is at the bottom.

**1.4 Females: Average Years of Healthy Life Expectancy at Birth, 2002**

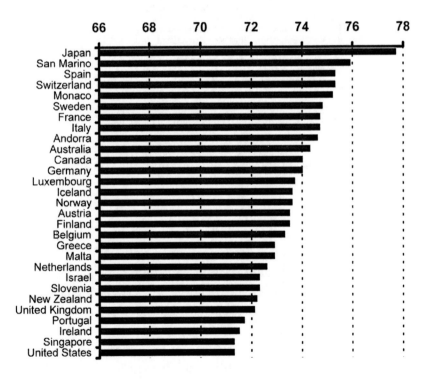

Data Source: *World Health Statistics 2006*, World Health Organization, Geneva, Switzerland.

## 1.5 Males: Average Years of Healthy Life Expectancy at Birth, 2002

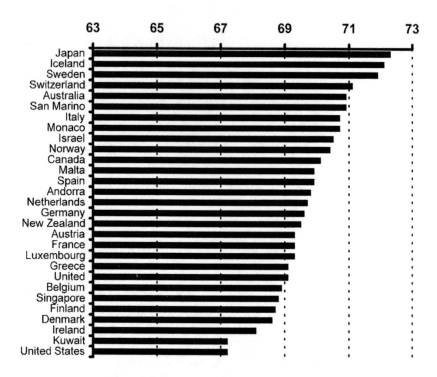

Data Source: *World Health Statistics 2006*, World Health Organization, Geneva, Switzerland.

Next, we will look at another way of examining the effectiveness of the medical system.

### Connecting Expenses and Health Results

To assess what level of value a nation is actually receiving for its medical investment, we can analyze the relationship between medical expenditures and health outcomes. For the greatest accuracy and reliability, it would be desirable to perform an in-depth cost-effectiveness analysis. This evaluation would be very complex and beyond the interest of most readers of this book. However, for a quick overview, let's look at an example.

ROBERT E. HERRON

1.6 Relationship of 2004 Total per Capita Expenditure on Health and Infant Deaths per 1,000 Live Births

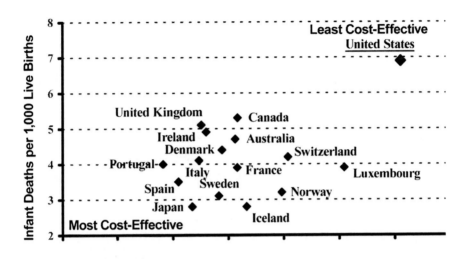

Total per Capita Expenditure on Health (U.S. Dollars)

Data Source: Organisation for Economic Co-operation and Development Health Data, 2006

Remember that because so many things must be done correctly within a medical system to achieve low infant mortality rates, it is a very sensitive and relatively comprehensive measure of system-wide effectiveness. In the previous chart on the vertical axis, we can see the 2004 infant mortality levels per 1,000 live births for selected developed nations with similar standards of living. On the horizontal axis we see the 2004 total per capita expenditure on health. We can see that Japan has the lowest infant death rate and the lowest per capita expenditure. In contrast, the United States has the highest infant mortality and the highest per capita expenditure. Thus, Japan appears to be receiving the best value for its medical investment, and the U.S. seems to be the least cost-effective. Most other nations fall in between these two extreme cases. Japan's low spending and superior maternal and infant health deserves further investigation to determine what is causing this phenomenon. There may be something occurring in Japan from which all nations' medical systems might learn to be more cost-effective.

## The Big Picture of U.S. Medical Cost-Effectiveness

Let's look at the entire American medical system's effectiveness by assessing its results and the money spent to obtain those outcomes during the last century. During the 1900-1950 period, U.S. life expectancy at birth increased 22 years. This improvement has been attributed by many researchers mainly to improved standard of living, public health, and preventive sanitation measures, such as improved water purity, hygiene, sewage treatment, food safety, and other non-medical interventions.[11-19] During this period, only 3% to 4 % of GNP was devoted to medical services. In the 1900-1950 era, there was almost no advanced medical technology upon which to spend vast sums of money.

In contrast, from 1950 to 2000 life expectancy increased by only 8 years in the United States, while spending on medical treatment rose from approximately 3.5% to over 15% of the GNP. In this period, there were many discoveries that resulted in the proliferation of expensive new medical technologies. The dominant focus was on the treatment of disease with the newest medical devices, surgery, and pharmaceuticals. As the funding for the high-technology medical system grew exponentially, public health and disease prevention funding waned.[20]

Thus, when the entire twentieth century is considered, improved standard of living, better economic conditions, sanitation, disease prevention, and health promotion seem to be a more cost-effective investment than high-technology medicine for improving population-wide health outcomes, such as life expectancy at birth.[11-19, 21] It would have been desirable to include an analysis of Healthy Life Expectancy at birth, but these data were unavailable for the early twentieth century. HALE records are relatively recent.

Comparing Life Expectancy at Birth and Percent of GNP Spent on Medical Services

1.7 Life Expectancy at Birth, 1900 - 2000

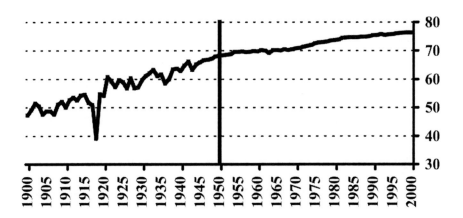

From 1900 to 1950, 22 years were gained, but from 1950 to 2000 only 8 years were gained.

Data Sources: Center for Disease Control and Prevention, Statistical Abstracts of the United States, and Historical Statistics of the United States: Colonial Times to 1970, part 1.

1.8 Percent of GNP Spent on Medical Care, 1900 - 2000

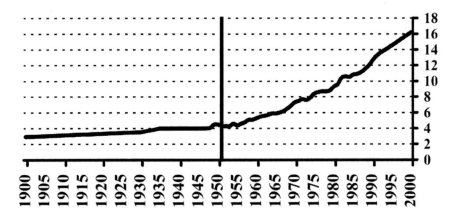

Data Sources: Center for Medicare and Medicaid Services, Health Care Financing Administration, Statistical Abstracts of the United States, and Historical Statistics of the United States: Colonial Times to 1970, part 1.

Other analyses have come to a similar conclusion. In a report titled *For a Healthy Nation: Returns on Investment in Public Health*, the U.S. Department of Health and Human Services and Public Health Service explained:

> Clinical medicine is credited with only five of the 30 years that have been added to life expectancy since the turn of the century (1900)....The majority of the gain has been achieved through improvements in our external environment—encompassing better nutrition, housing, sanitation, and occupational safety.[22]

We could probe even further to examine the long-term impact of modern medicine.

### The Law of Diminishing Returns: Spending More, Receiving Less

One would logically expect that as more money is spent on medical care, health improvements would correspondingly increase. Yet, there are limits, and inevitably investments reach a *point of diminishing returns*. "Diminishing returns" is an unhappy situation in which increases in spending bring less dramatic increases in health outcomes or results. The law of diminishing returns suggests that the rate of health improvements will fail to keep up with the rate of medical spending increases. We pay more to receive less. This law seems to be analogous to the second law of thermodynamics in physics, which posits that systems inevitably move from orderly states to disorderly ones, unless something is done to create additional order to overcome the tendency towards dissipation and entropy. New advanced medical discoveries and technologies were supposed to make medicine more effective than in the past, and thus overcome the trend towards diminishing returns. Let's consider a couple of examples that reflect what occurred in the entire medical system during the last century.

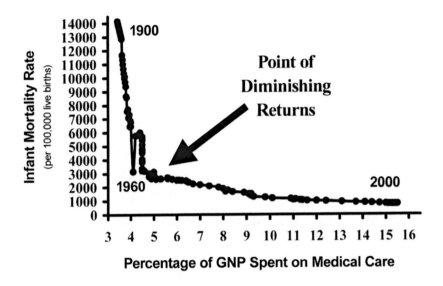

**Percentage of GNP Spent on Medical Care**

Data Sources: Center for Disease Control and Prevention, Center for Medicare and Medicaid Services, Health Care Financing Administration, Statistical Abstracts of the United States, and Historical Statistics of the United States: Colonial Times to 1970, part 1.

In the previous chart we see that from 1900 to 1960, the U.S. infant mortality rate declined steeply for a relatively small investment (3.5% to 6% of GNP). In the early 1960s, however, the United States reached its point of diminishing returns. After the early 1960s, we see that the medical investment increased dramatically from 6% to over 15% of GNP in 2000, but the rate of improvements in infant mortality slowed greatly when compared with the earlier reductions.

From 1900 to 1960, the total death rate declined steeply for a relatively little outlay (3.5% to 6% of GNP). Again, in the early 1960s the United States reached its point of diminishing returns. After the early 1960s, we see that medical spending jumped from 6% to over 15% of GNP in 2000, but the decline in total death rate slowed dramatically relative to the earlier large reductions. The following chart (1.10) on total death rate shows a similar trend.

## 1.10 Total Death Rate and GNP Spent on Medical Care, 1900 - 2000

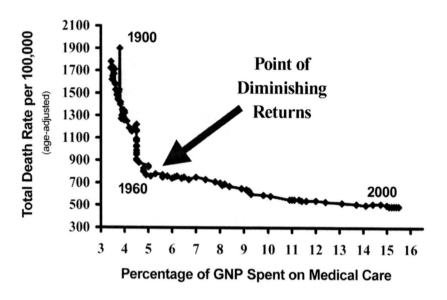

Data Sources: Center for Disease Control and Prevention, Center for Medicare and Medicaid Services, Health Care Financing Administration, Statistical Abstracts of the United States, and Historical Statistics of the United States: Colonial Times to 1970, part 1.

### The Advanced Technology Paradox

The paradox is that new technologies are supposed to increase effectiveness and not reduce it. Past research has shown that if there is an actual improvement in technology, the law of diminishing returns can be delayed.[23] In other industries, great enhancements in technology have prevented the diminishing returns phenomenon from occurring for long periods. Medicine is the exception. Biomedicine's diminishing returns began in the early 1960s, which coincidentally was the period when its greatest expansion of high-technology use started to accelerate. This trend continues today.

Due to the advanced medical technologies, there should have been at least continued declines in infant and total mortality rates similar to the earlier 1900-1960 era. When considering that the advanced technologies were proclaimed to be better than previous methods, one might even anticipate more steep reductions in mortality rates than in

ROBERT E. HERRON

the past. Surprisingly, instead of a quantum leap in improved national health outcomes and increased longevity, there was a major slow down or decrease in the rate of progress. In spite of the constant media hype over "miracle cures," we need to consider whether mod-

> **In other industries, great enhancements in technology have prevented the diminishing returns phenomenon from occurring for long periods. Medicine is the exception.**

ern medicine may be much less effective than most people believe. Timothy H. Holtz and colleagues have given a historical example of how little modern medicine has actually impacted health. During the 1800s and early 1900s, tuberculosis was the number one cause of death in many developed nations. Dr. Holtz explains:

> Mortality data for England and Wales show that the death rate for tuberculosis had already fallen by half during the 40 years before Koch discovered the bacillus. During the next 60 years, it fell by more than half again before effective chemotherapy (streptomycin) was introduced. Decreasing morbidity and mortality rates reflected improved living conditions.[24]

Dr. Aaron Wildavsky, Dean of the Graduate School of Public Policy, University of California Berkeley, has summarized the problem, including areas that we have not yet addressed:

> According to the great equation, Medical Care equals Health. But the Great Equation is wrong. More available medical care does not equal better health. The best estimates are that the medical system (doctors, drugs, hospitals) affects about 10 percent of the usual indices for measuring health.... The remaining 90 percent are determined by factors over which doctors have little or no control, from individual life style (smoking, exercise, worry), to social conditions (income, eating habits, physiological inheritance), to the physical environment (air and water quality). Most of the bad things that happen to people are at present beyond the reach of medicine.[25]

In a large study of U.S. Medicare enrollees, John E. Wennberg, Elliot S. Fisher, and colleagues found that higher medical spending did not result in more effective care or better health outcomes.[26-28] Amazingly, most proposals for medical system reform involve finding new ways to raise even more money to spend on the medical status quo. This chapter presented evidence suggesting that this approach may be unwise.

We really need to take a critical look at what value we are receiving for the soaring investment in medical systems worldwide. Why do nations and corporations pour ever-increasing amounts of money into medical systems that are yielding decreasing beneficial results? Perhaps there is a lack of knowledge.

> **Higher medical spending did not result in more effective care or better national health. However, most proposals for reform involve new ways to raise additional money to pay for the medical status quo.**

# Chapter 2

# Amend the Medical Theory to
# Save the Health System

*"In science, a model is revised or abandoned when it fails to account adequately for all the data. A dogma, on the other hand, requires that discrepant data be forced to fit the model or be excluded."*

—George L. Engel, M.D.[1]

## 2.1 Knowledge is the Basis of Action

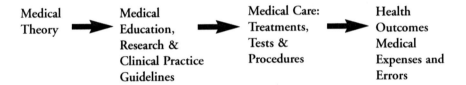

| Medical Theory | Medical Education, Research & Clinical Practice Guidelines | Medical Care: Treatments, Tests & Procedures | Health Outcomes Medical Expenses and Errors |

Is the predominant medical model based mainly on dogma or real scientific principles? In this chapter, we will present a new perspective for understanding medical systems, discuss the crucial role of knowledge in guiding health systems, review what the current medical theory is and where it came from, and explain why current medical knowledge must be amended or replaced to reform the health care systems of the world.

Medical theory and knowledge are like a map that guides almost every aspect of the health care system. A good map can make the difference between life and death in certain situations. For example, from October 1967 to November 1968, I served as an infantryman in the

U.S. Marine Corps in what was then called South Vietnam. My battalion was stationed mainly near the Demilitarized Zone (DMZ). We conducted operations to block the North Vietnamese Army from entering South Vietnam. We were in almost constant danger of being attacked. We used maps extensively to guide our patrols and other activities. In the western DMZ near the Laotian border, there were no natural boundaries. Thick jungle covered wild sprawling mountains, and navigation was difficult. Often, we could only see a few feet in front of us. The only maps to guide us were derived from those made by the French during their occupation of Indochina many years before we came. The original French maps may have been reliable, but the heavy rains from the annual monsoons eroded and altered the landscape in too many places. The old French charts had become obsolete. Inaccurate maps put us in danger. For instance, in one of our first operations in the western DMZ, a Marine helicopter dropped my squad of over a dozen men far from the rest of our unit. This unplanned separation was very hazardous. Because our map was faulty, we had no idea where we were. After realizing that we were in North Vietnam, we scrambled to get back into the DMZ. Not only was our little squad in danger of being attacked by vastly larger North Vietnamese regiments, but we could have also created an international incident that may have embarrassed the U.S. government. How would President Johnson explain the charges from other nations and the world press that Marines had "invaded" North Vietnam against orders? This mistake was due to inaccurate knowledge. In certain ways, modern medicine is similar to the western DMZ. Like thick jungle and rough mountains, complexity and uncertainty make too many treatments, tests, and other activities potentially hazardous. In this complicated and difficult terrain, medical professionals need a good map, or comprehensive knowledge, which can make the difference between life and death for many of their patients.

When it was formulated many years ago, the current medical model may have been fairly useful when considering the level of scientific understanding available. However, new discoveries in numerous non-medical disciplines, such as quantum physics, chaos theory, self-organizing systems, general systems, and other fields, have dramatically altered the knowledge landscape and how we understand nature and health. Medicine has neglected incorporating many of these important changes for decades. The current dictums of mind-body separation, reductionism, reliance on objective methods, and physical fundamentalism seem out of date in light of these new findings. For instance, physical fundamentalism is the belief that only matter is the basis of all structures and functions in humans, including the mind. All mental and subjective phenomena, including awareness itself, are thought to be byproducts of various physical mechanisms, such as the electro-chemical interactions in the brain and central nervous system. Yet, according to the most advanced understanding in quantum physics, at the deepest level, physical matter is a fluctuation of the underlying superstring field or unified field, and not only made of particles, which can be observed at more superficial levels. The unified field is the source of the universe, including the fundamental force and matter fields. Most basically, our human body is a set of waves or vibrations, not hard matter. This fact has important implications for the research and development of innovative medical treatments that are currently underappreciated and neglected. Like the eroding landscape of the western DMZ, modern medicine's map no longer matches the current scientific terrain. Thus, high-technology medicine, like the Marine helicopter pilot, may be misguided by old knowledge. The lack of completely accurate maps, or fundamental medical theory and related knowledge, could put us all in unnecessary danger.

The most extreme example of faulty knowledge is the failure of the underlying medical theory. Theory Failure occurs when systematic knowledge can not accurately, reliably, and comprehensively describe and explain

> Theory Failure occurs when systematic knowledge can not accurately, reliably, and comprehensively describe and explain phenomena within a field.

phenomena within a field. The ability of a model to precisely predict phenomena is evidence that its understanding is correct. Modern medicine may be suffering from at least a mild case of Theory Failure. To start, because knowledge guides systems, we will briefly present an innovative and comprehensive view of how medical systems function and how medical theory influences their effectiveness.

## General Systems and Subsystems

*"A system is a set of parts coordinated to accomplish a set of goals."*
—C. W. Churchman[2]

General Systems Theory has been a standard tool for understanding complex systems in a wide range of disciplines. General Systems Theory has been defined in various ways. The definition provided by E. S. Dacher is easily understood:

> Systems theory is an attempt to integrate, to create wholes out of parts. It is in essence a science of wholeness. Its concepts and principles are based on the observation that nature is organized in patterns of increasing complexity and comprehensiveness, and that these larger wholes, or units, have characteristics and qualities unique to the whole and cannot be identified or accessed through an analysis of their component parts.[3]

The parts of a system are usually grouped into subsystems that are functionally and structurally related or similar. This grouping facilitates analysis and synthesis of factors to better understand holistic functioning. Within the General Systems discipline, there are many possible ways of viewing and modeling any system's behavior. The following diagram shows the most basic system.

### 2.2 Most Fundamental General System

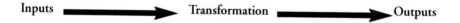

Inputs ⟶ Transformation ⟶ Outputs

Of course, the large medical system of a technologically advanced nation would have to be characterized by a richer diagram to fully appreciate how it functions. This is shown in the following chart.

## 2.3 Comprehensive General Systems Overview of the Medical Sector

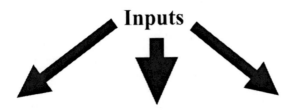

# Inputs

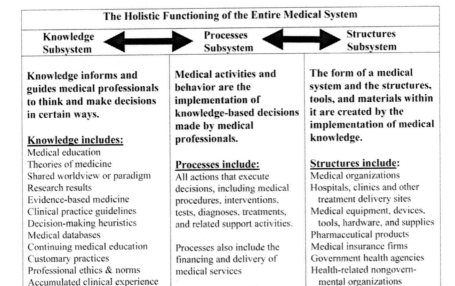

| The Holistic Functioning of the Entire Medical System | | |
|---|---|---|
| **Knowledge Subsystem** | **Processes Subsystem** | **Structures Subsystem** |
| Knowledge informs and guides medical professionals to think and make decisions in certain ways.<br><br>**Knowledge includes:**<br>Medical education<br>Theories of medicine<br>Shared worldview or paradigm<br>Research results<br>Evidence-based medicine<br>Clinical practice guidelines<br>Decision-making heuristics<br>Medical databases<br>Continuing medical education<br>Customary practices<br>Professional ethics & norms<br>Accumulated clinical experience | Medical activities and behavior are the implementation of knowledge-based decisions made by medical professionals.<br><br>**Processes include:**<br>All actions that execute decisions, including medical procedures, interventions, tests, diagnoses, treatments, and related support activities.<br><br>Processes also include the financing and delivery of medical services | The form of a medical system and the structures, tools, and materials within it are created by the implementation of medical knowledge.<br><br>**Structures include:**<br>Medical organizations<br>Hospitals, clinics and other treatment delivery sites<br>Medical equipment, devices, tools, hardware, and supplies<br>Pharmaceutical products<br>Medical insurance firms<br>Government health agencies<br>Health-related nongovernmental organizations |
| *Knowledge is basis of action* | *Processes integrate knowledge and structures* | *Form follows function* |

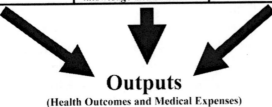

# Outputs
**(Health Outcomes and Medical Expenses)**

All of the parts of a system are grouped into subsystems to form an integrated whole. The medical system can be evaluated as three subsystems: knowledge, processes, and structures (shown in preceding figure 2.3). Past health reform efforts that have applied the General Systems approach focused mainly on the processes and structures subsystems of the medical system. These two were assumed to be the most important. However, this supposition is incorrect.

The organizing power of knowledge is important because it is the basis of action and results in any system. In its various forms, knowledge influences and guides almost all medical activities and organizational structures. Because it guides the coordination of parts and direction of the whole system, the knowledge subsystem is the most essential. Of course, other factors also influence medical professionals' decision making. However, the underlying foundational knowledge is primary. Thus, the knowledge subsystem is the most important one.

The knowledge subsystem includes: Theories and models of medicine, shared worldview or paradigm, decision-making heuristics, medical research results, clinical practice guidelines, all levels of medical education, medical organizational culture, professional ethics and norms, and other sources of knowledge that guide the activities of medical professionals. The knowledge imparted in medical schools is especially important because it helps to train health care professionals to think and make decisions in certain ways throughout their careers.

The primacy of knowledge in a system is verified in many disciplines. For example, Information Theory is a branch of mathematics that integrates knowledge from communications, engineering, physics, biology, and many other areas of learning. Information Theory explores and applies those laws of mathematics that govern the behavior of information when it is used in various ways. Information Theory posits that knowledge has organizing power.

The organizing power inherent in complete knowledge can transform an ineffective system into an efficient and cost-effective one. In contrast, incomplete knowledge can cause failure in even the most well-funded system with the best-intentioned professionals. To obtain better health results, more comprehensive knowledge must be acquired and applied than in the past. Today, most medical research is not developing the holistic knowledge that is needed to produce improved system-wide results. This must change.

With regard to medical professionals, a principle of the general systems approach is that the overall performance of a system does not necessarily indicate whether the people within it are doing their jobs well or poorly. It is possible for highly trained people to give their best individual performance while the system as a whole produces less than optimal results. The system is the main problem. When excellent people try to function in a severely flawed system, the systemic difficulties can negate the individual contributions of even the most sincere, dedicated, and competent medical professionals.

## Theoretical Foundations of Modern Medicine

We will briefly review the theoretical foundations of biomedicine. The terms modern medicine and biomedicine (i.e., medicine based on biological and related sciences) are used interchangeably. Then, we will review some of the major objections and anomalies related to the medical model. Dr. Derick Wade and Dr. Peter Halligan[4] of the United Kingdom have listed the main foundational beliefs of modern medicine as:

- "All illness and all symptoms arise from an underlying abnormality within the body (usually in the functioning or structure of specific organs), referred to as a disease.

- All diseases give rise to symptoms.

- Health is the absence of disease.

- Mental phenomena are separate from and unrelated to other disturbances of bodily function.

- The patient is a victim of circumstance with little or no responsibility for the presence or cause of the illness.

The patient is a passive recipient of treatment, although cooperation with treatment is expected."[4]

In addition, Dr. John Abramson[5] who teaches primary care at Harvard Medical School has further explained:

"The unspoken underlying narrative of biomedicine shared by most doctors today can be summed up by four principles:

- The origin of disease is best sought at the smallest level of function, usually molecular, genetic, and cellular.

- Dysfunction at the molecular level causes dysfunction at progressively higher levels of function.

- The most effective medical care is focused on individual patients.

- The challenges of medicine are adequately and completely addressed by the objective methods of science."[5]

These basic principles underlie and guide almost all biomedical activities worldwide. These precepts are so much a part of the medical culture and worldview that few within the system would ever think to question them.

> When one is considering systems, it's always wise to raise questions about the most obvious and simple assumptions.[2]
>
> —C. W. Churchman

Since the earliest days of their education, medical professionals have generally assumed that all or most of the previous points are correct. From where did these foundational concepts come?

*The body is a machine, so built up and composed of nerves, muscles, veins, blood and skin, that though there were no mind in it at all, it would not cease to have the same functions.*

—René Descartes (1596–1650), *Traité de l'Homme*

René Descartes, Friedrich Hoffmann, and others established the foundations of our current biomedical theory. They based their medical paradigm on seventeenth-century science, which was the most advanced knowledge available to them. Early scientists Galileo and Newton explained that the universe was a vast machine, like a huge mechanical clock. Descartes and others applied this idea to medicine and proposed that the human body also functions like a machine, illness is a breakdown in the machine, and the doctor is the repairman.

The model of Descartes had certain advantages and disadvantages. This machine analogy led to numerous advances and discoveries that helped to improve the health and standard of living for the entire planet.

Several researchers modified Descartes' medical theory in the mid-nineteenth century to expand our understanding of the mechanisms of disease. They applied the principles of scientific experimentation to make great discoveries that shaped the biomedical model into its current form. Yet, most of its basic seventeenth-century tenets remained almost the same. Louis Pasteur published the first paper on germ theory in 1857. From Pasteur, Joseph Lister derived the principles that enabled him to introduce the antiseptic doctrine that reduced infections during surgery. The development of vaccination by Edward Jenner and others helped to further shape the theory.

Research on infection by Louis Pasteur, Robert Koch, and their adherents led to the doctrine of the specific etiology, which posits that each disorder has only one most important cause. If this cause can be neutralized or eliminated, then health will be restored.

**2.4 Biomedical Model of Causality: The Doctrine of Specific Etiology**

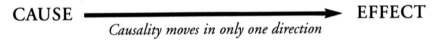

CAUSE ⟶ EFFECT
*Causality moves in only one direction*

single microbe,
defective gene,
cellular imbalance,
or injury

one disease or
disorder

This is also called the "one cause one effect" model, which guides modern medicine.

This doctrine was integrated into all areas of medicine and is probably the most salient feature of the biomedical paradigm. This one cause one effect model worked extremely well in helping to eliminate infectious diseases, which were the main cause of death during the 1800s. Paul Ehrlich, Gerhard Domagk, Selman Waksman, Alexander Fleming and others helped to develop antibiotics and pharmacology as the basis of modern therapeutics. In keeping with the tenets of specific etiology, Rudolf Virchow established the principle that almost all diseases arise from cellular imbalances or abnormalities. Dr. Virchow also emphasized that the social, non-medical determinants of health must be addressed, but this suggestion was generally ignored by mainstream medicine. The doctrine of the single etiology inspired a similar development in pharmacology: the single active ingredient theory. The basic idea is that one most important ingredient in a medication will address the single cause of a disease. Next, we need to consider the modern understanding of health.

## Health Defined

The changing definition of the word *health* gives us insights into the development of the biomedical model. The word health comes from the Old English base *hal*, which is also the root of the word "whole." Health literally means whole or the state of wholeness. Many holistic definitions of health have been postulated throughout history. Since earliest Greek times, health was regarded as a state of dynamic equilibrium (balance) within the individual and between the individual and environment. This equilibrium was achieved when people lived in harmony with themselves and with their environment. Ancient Greek concepts of health influenced the Romans and persisted in western civilization in some form until the middle 1800s.[6] The objective was to maintain a dynamic state of balance by living in tune with nature. However, this nature-oriented view of health contrasts greatly with the current machine model of modern medicine.

An important point is that biomedicine has no clear definition of health. Thus, by default health is assumed to be the absence of clinically detectable disease, imbalance, or injury. Modern medicine has generally avoided a definition because medical professionals have mainly focused on treating and studying diseases.[7] As Dr. C. Whitbeck has explained:

> Until recently, the term "health" was hardly mentioned in medical circles—the term does not even appear in the index of many standard medical texts.... Then, the only danger of conceptual confusion

regarding health arose from the attempt to define health entirely in terms of medical concepts, such as those of disease and injury. This attempt generated the so-called "negative notion" of health, health as the absence of disease, injury, and impairment. The term "health," however, was only rarely used in this way. Even in such expressions as "restoring the patient to health," "health" often does not mean "the absence of disease." Instead, "restoring the patient to health" merely means restoring the patient to a pre-morbid level of functioning where "pre-morbid" refers only to a particular episode of illness, so that the "health" of the "restored" patient still includes all his or her chronic diseases as well as poor physical condition, neurotic malaise, and so forth.[7]

A definition of health must serve theoretical needs (describe, explain and predict), and it must also be practical enough to use in day-to-day clinical treatment to direct resources to achieve the desired health outcomes. Theory and practice support each other. A clear, precise, and practical definition of health is an important part of the "map" or knowledge subsystem that should be guiding medical systems.

Health is the goal of medical systems. If one desires to attain any goal, it first must be defined clearly. Then, we can devise the means to achieve the goal. Achievement of an indefinite goal is usually difficult, and often impossible. We have seen that the old medical models generally defined health as a state of the holistic and integrated balance of mind, body, behavior, and environment. In contrast, modern medicine has defined health in terms of the absence of clinically measurable symptoms.

The definition of health, or the lack of one, is important because it would determine the goal or target of the entire medical system. This definition influences how medical systems are organized and how health sector funds are allocated. Generally, the clinical detection of disease, injury, or imbalance activates the system to "fix" the broken machine. Thus, the current approach to health helps to channel most funds towards treatment and away from much-needed disease prevention and health promotion. Due to the principle of reductionism, medicine has lost its original focus on wholeness and has become lost in the parts.

## The Reductionist Approach

Reductionism is an essential component of current medical research, practice, and theory.

**2.5 The Reductionist Strategy for Obtaining Knowledge: Analyze Parts to Understand and Control Whole**

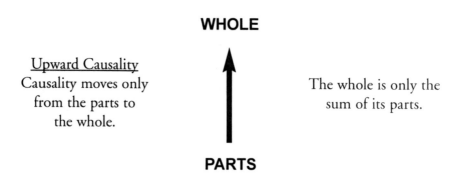

**WHOLE**

Upward Causality
Causality moves only
from the parts to
the whole.

The whole is only the
sum of its parts.

**PARTS**

This approach to gaining knowledge is also common to most of modern science. René Descartes proposed that all phenomena could be known by *reducing* them to their constituent parts. This strategy requires the systematic breaking down of a complex problem into smaller, more fundamental parts. Evaluation of the parts is supposed to yield information about the whole that will eventually produce solutions. This approach has worked well for many types of mathematical, scientific, engineering, and medical problems. Thus, medicine examines increasingly smaller parts of the physiology to gain knowledge of the whole. Today, the main focus is on genes, molecules, and cellular mechanisms. Medical researchers use this information to develop more effective treatments to fight disease. The most popular strategy is to develop genetic and molecular interventions to cure the apparent causes of disease. Great progress has been made with the reductionist strategy. However, from many recent discoveries we suspect that this approach alone may be incomplete.

When compared with other disciplines modern medicine is remarkably fragmented in its knowledge, processes, and structure subsystems. Fragmentation is important because it tends to cause confusion and chaos within a system. This fragmentation is mainly due to the principle of reductionism that focuses on the parts, and too often neglects the whole. An aid to gaining complete knowledge would be to alternate steps of comprehensive analysis and synthesis. Comprehensive means that we include all relevant details to facilitate a thorough understanding. We must repeatedly question our most basic assumptions and reconsider all data to determine whether they fit with the current theories or not.

### 2.6 An Aid in the Acquisition of Complete Knowledge

ANALYSIS (PARTS) ←————————→ SYNTHESIS (WHOLE)

**The acquisition of knowledge must include constant alternation and comprehensive integration of both analysis and synthesis.**

Biomedicine is extensively applying analysis, which is defined as the process of separating or breaking a whole into its constituent parts, and then examining these parts. On the other hand, synthesis is the process of putting together the parts to form a whole. By continuously alternating comprehensive analysis and synthesis, we can enhance our ability to describe, understand, and explain phenomena as a complete whole. This process needs to be consistently applied to all subsystems in an integrated manner.

Complete knowledge does not mean increased complexity. Sometimes when a new discovery is made, complexity might seem to be increased in the short term, because the new information raises more questions than it answers. This happens because we do not yet know the full story in that area. An incomplete understanding is usually the source of excessive complexity, which creates confusion and chaos. A deep understanding of a field means moving in the direction of increased unification and simplicity. The medical sciences desperately need to be simplified and unified. Dr. Albert Einstein has explained, "If you can't explain it simply, you don't understand it well enough."

On the practical clinical level, fragmentation tends to create additional steps of testing and treatment that may be unnecessary. These increased steps require extensive communication and coordination, which raises the likelihood of lapses that will cause medical errors, undesirable outcomes, and increased expenses. As complete knowledge is gained through alternating steps of analysis and synthesis, medicine will be able to unify, consolidate, integrate, and simplify its knowledge, processes, and structures subsystems. When this is accomplished, there will be fewer and more effective steps of treatment with reduced errors and negative side effects, reduced costs, and increased patient satisfaction. Not all health care professionals agree with the biomedical model.

## Objections to the Dominant Medical Model

Some medical professionals have growing doubts about the accuracy of the knowledge that guides most aspects of the medical system. For instance, Dr. Nancy Krieger explained:

> Opening up new ways of seeing the world, metaphors can both help and hinder understanding. Consider, for example, the metaphor of "man-as-machine," as developed by Descartes. On the one hand, this metaphor led to new scientific knowledge by spurring non-vitalistic explanations of human biology. At the same time, its inherent mind/body dualism and reductionism has blocked and continues to hinder research on psychosocial determinants of health.[8]

There have been numerous challenges to the theoretical foundations of modern medicine.[1,3,4,9-12] We will briefly review some of the most important points. Dr. George L. Engel, a former professor of psychiatry and medicine at the University of Rochester School of Medicine, published an article in *Science* in 1977 titled, "The Need for a New Medical Model: A Challenge for Biomedicine."[1] This article started an insurgency to transform modern medicine that continues today. Dr. Engel explained his main objection to biomedicine:

> I contend that all medicine is in crisis and, further, that medicine's crisis derives from the same basic fault as psychiatry's, namely, adherence to a model of disease no longer adequate for the scientific tasks and social responsibilities of either medicine or psychiatry.... Medicine's

crisis stems from the logical inference that since "disease" is defined in terms of somatic parameters, physicians need not be concerned with psychosocial issues which lie outside medicine's responsibility and authority.[1]

Dr. Engel challenged modern medicine to expand its worldview and area of responsibility to adopt what he called the Biopsychosocial Model. Yet, mainstream medicine has generally resisted his suggested improvements.

In recent years, there have been many other challenges to the precepts of the reigning medical theory.[9-12] For instance, Dr. Derick Wade and Dr. Peter Halligan have explained:

> The biomedical model of illness, which has dominated health care for the past century, cannot fully explain many forms of illness. This failure stems partly from three assumptions: all illness has a single underlying cause, disease (pathology) is always the single cause, and removal or attenuation of the disease will result in a return to health. Evidence exists that all three assumptions are wrong.[4]

Dr. I.R. McWhinney has further elaborated:

> As empirical research continues to produce results that are anomalies in the dominant mechanistic paradigm, the time for a change in paradigm —in the Khunian sense—draws nearer. Eventually, it will become intolerable to have a theory of medicine that cannot accommodate the evidence for the effect on health of the meaning of experience, expectations, beliefs, intentionality, and relationships.[13]

These are just a very small sample of the views of medical professionals who have serious doubts about the dominant medical model. There are also other ways of documenting the inadequacy of biomedicine.


### Mistakes versus Efficiency

Mistake or error rates are an important factor in evaluating the efficiency and effectiveness of any system. We observe that medical errors are rampant in the current system. In most industries, such as airlines or manufacturers, mistakes provide clues to overall efficiency. If the biomedical model is accurate and complete, why do we have an epidemic of errors and negative treatment side effects worldwide?

In 1999, the Institute of Medicine (IOM) of the U.S. National Academy of Sciences published a report, *To Err Is Human: Building a Safer Health System*. This report reviewed the research on medical errors.[14] The IOM found "More people die in a given year as a result of medical errors than from motor vehicle accidents (43,458), breast cancer (42,297), or AIDS (16,516)."[14] Robert M. Wachter, M.D. and Kaveh G. Shojania, M.D. have further commented:

> The rash of clinical mistakes we call our "epidemic of errors" is simply the latest sign that something is dangerously wrong beneath the shining veneer of modern medicine.[15]

In a survey of 2,012 adults in the United States, the Kaiser Family Foundation found that 34% of respondents reported that they or a family member had been a victim of a medical error at some time during their lives.[16] Of those who had a chronic medical condition, 50% said they or a family member experienced a medical error. Of those who suffered serious medical errors, only 1 in 7 said they initiated a malpractice lawsuit. More than half of those surveyed said they were dissatisfied with the quality of medical care and that the quality of medical services in the U.S. has become worse in recent years.[16] According to this poll, 92% of the respondents said serious medical errors should be required to be reported to the public and not kept secret.[16]

In late 2003, Dr. Gary Null and colleagues completed a comprehensive review of medical journals and government reports that evaluated all of the ways the medical system contributes to injury, illness, and death in the United States.[17] They presented extensive scientific evidence to suggest that the medical system itself is the number one cause of death in the U.S.[17] According to another study published in 2000, Dr. Starfield of Johns Hopkins University estimated that 250,000 deaths each year are caused by various aspects of medical treatment in the United States. This estimate would make medical mistakes the third-largest cause of death behind heart disease and cancer.[18, 19]

Academic researchers may debate whether medical errors, negative drug side effects, and other factors together are the number one, three, or sixth cause of death in the U.S. However, for most people the bottom line is that the injuries, fatalities, and high bills from medical errors, omissions, and treatment side effects persist at unacceptably high levels. All of this unintended harm suggests that at least part of the current body of medical knowledge may be ineffective.

## Failure to Cure Chronic Diseases

If a man buys a dog for hunting, and after an excursion chasing game, he finds: "this dog can't hunt," naturally he gets a better canine for his next hunting trip. What, then, would we do with a medical model that can't cure? Chronic diseases are disorders that have become long lasting,

> The "one cause one effect" model of modern medicine fails to describe and explain multi-causal disorders, including most chronic diseases. This fact may be the reason these disorders have remained "incurable."

because biomedicine has no cure for them, only alleviation of some symptoms. Research has found that approximately 45% of the U.S. population—over 100 million people—suffer from at least one chronic disease.[20] In the United States, chronic disorders also account for at least 75% of national medical expenditures.[20] If chronic diseases are a major problem, why has modern medicine failed to cure them? How could such a lapse occur in the age of advanced, high-technology "miracle cure" medicine?

We recall the doctrine of the specific etiology or "one cause one effect" model, which worked so well for containing, reducing, and even eliminating many infectious diseases. Because it was so successful in the past, this model is still the predominant map for understanding disease causality. However, research has shown that most chronic diseases, such as cancers and cardiovascular disorders, are extremely complex and appear to have numerous contributing factors. Biomedicine has had difficulty handling multi-causal disorders, because they do not fit with the "one cause one effect" model that still strongly influences the medical system.

Thus, the many contributors to chronic diseases are labeled "risk factors." The current theory predicts that with enough research the single, underlying "cause" will eventually be found, probably a genetic disorder. Is it reasonable to assume that all diseases will always have one single cause?

In any system there is a relationship between all the parts. The sum of all the parts and their interrelationships forms a unique entity, or whole. This whole is different from any part or group of parts, including the set of all the parts. Each part also has a relation with the whole, and this relationship is also included in the wholeness that is more than the sum of the parts. Every cell has a relationship with every other cell in the human body because they can communicate through several means such as neuropeptides, growth factors, and hormones.

Biomedicine's adherence to its narrow model seems to be why these chronic diseases have remained incurable. Dr. René Dubos, a most distinguished medical research scientist, explained:

> In reality, however, search for *the* cause may be a hopeless pursuit because most disease states are the indirect outcome of a constellation of circumstances rather than the direct result of single determinant factors.[6]

The Director of the U.S. National Institutes of Health, Dr. Elias Zerhouni, has further explained: "You need new tools for understanding biology as systems. We need to get away from the reductionist approach: One gene or one event causes disease."[21]

## Gene Therapy and Biotechnology

The problems of biotechnology are also a troubling anomaly. From this "one cause one effect" viewpoint, health is defined as an intact genome (i.e., complete set of chromosomes). The genome was hypothesized to be the single all-powerful controller of every aspect of our physical structure and functioning. Gene therapy is the replacement or repair of defective genetic material to restore health. It was hailed as a miracle cure. However, several research projects had to be stopped because gene therapy harmed or killed patients.[22]

Biotechnology needs to review its underlying assumptions. Although one dysfunctional gene or molecule can make a person sick, no one gene, chromosome, or other fundamental part of the human physiology alone can make a person healthy. Human health requires that all levels of the body are balanced and function well. Very few disorders involve only one genetic cause. Genetic interventions have been unsuccessful in treating many genes simultaneously in a patient. Thus, most human diseases are not amenable to genetic remedies. Chronic diseases generally involve multiple genetic components.

Recent research shows that exercise, diet, and numerous environmental factors can modify gene expression and change the functioning of the most basic genetic components.[23-29] This means that the genome is not the sole all-omnipotent controller of human health that it was once believed to be. Because behavioral and environmental factors can modify gene expression,[23-29] and because of the inherent technical limitations of biotechnology, gene therapy is unlikely to be completely safe and effective, and it may never produce the medical miracles that have been promised by some prominent scientists and hyped by the media. There are other factors that influence health.

## Socioeconomic Status, Education, Social Standing, and Other Non-Medical Determinants of Health

There are important non-medical determinants of health, including socioeconomic status, education, position within an organization/society (social standing), and social support. The majority of the danger to longevity is due to these factors.[30-36] Research by Dr. Michael Marmot in Great Britain and colleagues has found that these non-medical variables are more accurate and reliable predictors of long-term health status and medical expenses than all physical or clinical measures of health combined.[31-36] For example, even when people have universal medical insurance and access to the same medical services, studies find wealthy people tend to be healthier, and low income people tend to be sicker.[31,32] There is also a consistent gradation in health at each level of socioeconomic status between the greatest extremes. This means progressively greater wealth and social standing yields correspondingly better health.[31,32] The current medical model fails to explain why socioeconomic status, social standing, and related factors influence mortality and morbidity more strongly than the physical variables that are the main focus of modern medicine and clinical practice.[31,32]

Another set of anomalies are those physical disorders that have mental or psychological origins—*psychosomatic diseases*. The very existence of psychosomatic maladies presents a very serious challenge to the validity of Descartes' dictums of mind-body separation and the reductionist principle that causality moves only from parts to whole. From clinical experience and a fairly large body of published studies, researchers have learned that a vast array of diseases are either aggravated or caused by mental phenomena, such as chronic psychological stress.[37, 38] For instance, chronic mental stress can weaken the immune system and make people more susceptible to physical diseases.[37-41] Psychosomatic diseases and the placebo effect challenge biomedicine's mind-body separation, reductionism, and belief that physical factors are the sole basis of pathology.

Even though most good physicians understand very well that mental phenomena can affect their patients' health, science and biomedicine have generally avoided answering the mind-body challenge. In spite of the growing evidence, medical systems apply mainly physical treatments, such as drugs and surgery. Medical professionals are expected to follow clinical practice guidelines that tend to focus mainly on the physical aspects of disease and neglect the psychological, social, and economic components. Commercial interests, of course, have played a role in this neglect. A dysfunctional medical model seems to have been very profitable for the Medical Industrial Complex.[42] Another reason may be that too many other essential beliefs, such as objectivity and medicine's methods of gaining knowledge, could also be called into question if mind-body separation, reductionism, and physical fundamentalism were weakened or dissolved. Then, most of modern medicine would be in doubt. So, while the numerous anomalies have been quietly addressed by some clinicians, what does this mean for the big picture?

## The Critical Need for a New Medical Theory

Anomalies, such as the global epidemic of incurable chronic diseases, suggest that the model or knowledge that guides modern medicine may be incomplete and at least partially erroneous. The predominant medical paradigm seems adequate for treating acute disorders, but not for chronic conditions. Since so much human suffering and the majority of medical expenditures are due to chronic diseases, it seems that updating the medical model to address these disorders should be a very high priority.

Today, our medical system is still strongly influenced by the seventeenth-century belief that the body is a machine, illness is a breakdown in the machine, and the doctor is the repairman. We are not machines governed by simple "one cause one effect" mechanisms. Research shows that human health and disease are extremely complex. Because the billions of cells in our body can communicate and interact in virtually infinite combinations and permutations, the causes of health and disease seem extremely complex. In addition, environmental factors can interact with cells to affect health status, which makes describing and explaining health even more complicated.

The failure of medical theory has led to the massive diversion of funding and other resources away from the actual determinants of human health. This diversion is caused mainly by the incomplete and obsolete medical model. Consequently, this faulty map appears to be the root cause of most of our health system problems. How would we remedy the misdirection of resources? The first step would be to amend or replace the dysfunctional medical theory with a simpler and more effective understanding of health.

# Innovative Solutions

In Chapter 3, we will show that a new medical model is emerging from the needs of the general population and the growth of complementary and alternative medicine. We will compare and contrast the old and new medical models.

In Chapter 4, we will present scientific research that has found that certain types of complementary and alternative medicine can both improve health and reduce medical costs.

In Chapter 5, we will present scientific research on an example of an innovative procedure for improving health and reducing medical expenses.

# Chapter 3

# Health and the New Medical Model

*"All models have a common defect. They are static. And as facts and circumstances change, models that were descriptive in an earlier phase in the evolution of a problem may be neither descriptive nor useful in later phases. Those who cling to an outmoded model of a problem become prisoners of their own formulations and unwittingly limit their ability to influence the conditions they wish to change."*

—Dr. Jeff Goldsmith [1]

We seem to be in the midst of a global transformation in the medical model. Many streams of knowledge and medical traditions are converging to re-shape medical care in the twenty-first century. What is causing this change? When the medical establishment ignores useful innovative contributions, biomedicine loses its leadership role. Consequently, a knowledge vacuum has been created and many alternative models are rushing to fill the void.

When leaders within a system perceive it to be successful, they tend to perpetuate those factors that led to their past successes. However, these factors may not lead to future success. Too often, medicine neglects or discards new ideas that do not fit with its old model. This tendency could "unwittingly limit their ability to influence the conditions they wish to change,"[1] such as reducing medical errors, high costs, unnecessary and ineffective treatments, and negative medication side effects.

In addition, Theory Failure misguides the allocation of medical resources in important ways. As mentioned previously, reductionism misguides clinicians and policy leaders to focus mainly on the parts: the smallest components of health, instead of the whole. Thus, millions of people worldwide feel that their health needs are not being fulfilled adequately. They desire a more comprehensive approach to health than biomedicine alone.

In response to the failure of medical theory, the people of this planet are trying to create safe and effective health systems. We see expressions of this change bubbling up in our neighborhood alternative medical facilities. People have minds of their own and seem to be re-structuring the medical paradigm mainly with their choices in the marketplace. For instance, a survey in 1997 found American adults paid $36 billion to $47 billion for their Complementary and Alternative Medicine (CAM) treatments.[2] Many of these people paid for their CAM care mainly with their own funds ($12.2 billion to $19.6 billion) without the help of medical insurance. Barnes et al. explained, "These fees are more than the U.S. public paid out-of-pocket for all hospitalizations in 1997 and about half that paid for all out-of-pocket physician services."[3] Clearly, the people are not entirely satisfied with the current health care system, so they are going elsewhere. This is a consumer-driven medical paradigm change.

### 3.1 New Global Integration of Medical Models

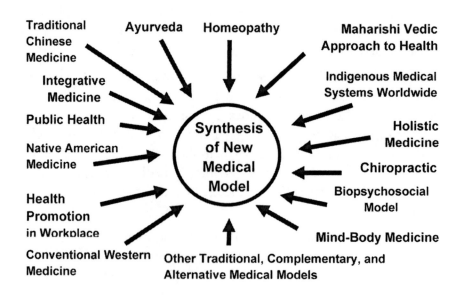

ROBERT E. HERRON

Many medical professionals support some aspects of the emerging paradigm. However, the mainstream of the Medical Industrial Complex still resists this popular movement, as evidenced by its efforts to thwart consumption of vitamins and natural supplements, block insurance coverage of CAM, and apparently stymie almost everything that does not fit with their medical paradigm (and profit needs).[4-7] Instead, they favor more drugs, surgery, radiation, and other biomedical interventions.[4-7] A few corporations, however, are buying into the emerging medical model for their own long-term profit as well as for their customers' health and happiness.

## Shared Traits Create New Paradigm

In the global interaction of medical models, an important observation is that most of these unconventional systems have many shared or overlapping characteristics and principles. They have similar goals, such as the holistic treatment of the patient and preservation of health through a balanced life in harmony with nature. They generally

> Although it is in the early stages of development, the emerging knowledge subsystem seems to represent a major revolution in the understanding of health that might help transform conventional medicine by stimulating its leaders to re-evaluate their most basic assumptions.

tend to give a higher priority to preventive strategies that focus on body, mind, spirit, and environment than acute sickness care, as in biomedicine. They have more in common that unites them than dissimilar precepts that might divide them. While all of these new entrants are competing for patients in the medical marketplace, they are unintentionally collaborating to help create a new medical paradigm—a scientific revolution toward a new understanding of health production.

The following table compares some of the traits of the Old Medical Model (biomedicine or conventional Western medicine) with those of the Emerging Medical Model, which consists of the generally shared characteristics of the new entrants into the medical marketplace.

We have seen that conventional Western medicine has defined

health in terms of the presence, or absence, of clinically measurable symptoms. In contrast, the emerging medical paradigm generally defines health as a state of the holistic and integrated balance of mind, body, behavior, and environment. This difference is important because the definition of health influences how medical systems are organized and how health sector funds are allocated. Although it is in the early stages of development, the emerging paradigm seems to represent a major revolution in the understanding of health that might help transform conventional medicine by stimulating its leaders to re-evaluate their most basic assumptions.

The emerging paradigm could help provide new, creative ideas for improving the outdated medical theory. In this scenario, the best of biomedicine and the best of the recent medical market entrants could be merged to provide a new, more comprehensive medical system. The unification of Descartes' mind-body dichotomy would be a useful step toward a new medical model. Of course, whatever direction medical professionals decide to take should be verified by rigorous scientific research.

### 3.2 The Old and Emerging Knowledge Subsystems Compared

| | *Old Medical Model*<br>(Biomedicine, Conventional Western Medicine) | *Emerging Medical Model*<br>(Traits shared among many new models) |
|---|---|---|
| **Conceptual Framework** | Cartesian-Newtonian machine model; everything is discrete and unrelated; parts are basis of whole; linear causal understanding; whole is only sum of parts | Unified model of health and Nature: self-referral, consciousness-based, dynamic, nonlinear, living system; everything is connected |
| **Scientific Validity** | Not consistent with most advanced scientific understandings of Nature; if quantum physics is true, most of "modern" medicine is out of date and has questionable scientific basis | Consistent with the most advanced scientific understanding of Nature, including quantum physics, chaos theory, general systems & self-organizing systems |
| **Basic Assumption** | Separation of mind and body; reductionism, physical fundamentalism; the molecular level of matter is the basis of life and consciousness; intact genes are main basis of health | Unity of mind, body, behavior, and environment; consciousness is basis of matter, body, and life; dynamic equilibrium of all factors is important for good health |
| **Health Definition** | Health is undefined, but it is assumed to be the absence of clinically detectable diseases, genetic defects, imbalances, or injuries | Health is the dynamic state of balance of human consciousness, mind, body, behavior, society, environment, and their interconnections |
| **Scientific Evaluation** | 80% to 85% of all medical treatments have no published, peer-reviewed research verifying effectiveness and safety | Approximately 95% of treatments in new models have no research showing they are effective and safe |

ROBERT E. HERRON

| Main Research Approach | Analysis: reductionism is the means to understand nature; break down body into parts; part is basis of whole; genetic level is best area to conduct medical research | Holistic approach: integration of analysis and synthesis; the whole is more than the sum of the parts and easier to understand and manage than the parts; holistic research approach |
|---|---|---|
| Treatment Strategies | Disease-oriented: suppress symptoms, destroy pathogens, replace defective organs and remove diseased tissues | Prevention-oriented: restore and maintain balance in individual and environment to prevent disease and promote health |
| Medical Education | Main focus on high-technology disease treatment; tends to give low priority to prevention, diet, lifestyle, geriatrics | Disease prevention and health promotion focus; aims to treat whole person and environment |
| Economic Impact | Increased expenditures; no reliable means to reduce long term costs | Reduced medical expenditures when applied comprehensively and consistently |
| Attitude Toward Nature | Forcefully manipulate and control Nature—Nature is chaotic and random (Nature and Mankind are adversaries) | Nature has infinite intrinsic order, creativity, and intelligence; balance, attunement, and harmony with Nature—Nature organizes best (Natural Law and Mankind are one) |
| Limitations | Maximum effectiveness in short term often with long-term adverse side effects. Ineffective at treating chronic illness. Neglects prevention and environmental, social, and psychological aspects of health | Maximum effectiveness in long term. Often too slow for immediate treatment of acute pathologies and emergency care situations |
| Curative Methods | Mechanical and Synthetic: High-technology treatment, synthetic pharmacology, surgery, chemotherapy, radiation, gene therapies, etc. | Organic: Natural treatments and prevention; restore balance holistically by lifestyle improvement, proper diet, meditation, stress reduction, exercise, herbs, etc. |
| Responsible for Health | Physician: clinician has medical care knowledge; information asymmetry gives medical doctor almost total control and responsibility | Patient has most responsibility; physician serves as a consultant and advisor. Individual is empowered with self-care knowledge to prevent disease and promote health |

## Working with Nature

One of the precepts shared among most of the emerging models is that to maintain health, we must live in tune with nature. The common understanding is that nature is maximally intelligent, creative, orderly, wholesome, nourishing, and powerful. Nature organizes best. Consequently, individual health is maintained by living in accord with nature's organizing principles or laws. Disease is seen as an individual's deviation from nature's dictums. For instance, improper diet, sleep deprivation, cigarette smoking, alcohol and drug abuse, and chronic stress damage health because nature did not design our physiologies to handle these activities. In addition, we should also consider large-scale health-damaging situations, such as excessive income disparity, environmental and food toxicity, and societal stress. Thus, all of these health-degrading phenomena could be called violations of natural law. This idea is not new. For example, Dr. Edward Jenner (1749 – 1823) explained in his essay titled *The Cow Pox*, "The deviation of Man from the state in which he was originally placed by Nature seems to have proved to him a prolific source of Disease."[8]

Efficiency in a medical system means collectively working with nature's organizing principles. On the other hand, if physicians and patients fail to be aware of and act in accord with these laws, the medical system could become very inefficient in producing health and incur high expenses. This view of efficiency is related to the Law of Least Action in the physical sciences. In modern physics, the Principles of Least Action and Conservation of Energy suggest that the underlying laws of nature that govern the universe are extremely efficient.[9] The precise movements of planets, solar systems, and galaxies are examples. This means nature is economical: nature is always doing the least to accomplish the most at all levels simultaneously.[9]

The Principle of Least Action is not limited to phenomena studied by physical scientists, but it is also pervasive throughout human activities. While much neglected, this principle is also an important aspect of man-made organizations. We can apply the Principle of Least Action to improve health care systems. How does a medical system do the least to accomplish the most like nature?

To produce an efficient medical system, the path of least action is to establish and maintain comprehensive, effective disease-prevention and health-promotion programs that are fully covered by medical insurance. Dr. Alexander Leaf gives a historical perspective:

> Medicine traditionally stands on two pillars: prevention and cure. For the past century the profession has rallied almost exclusively under the banner of curative medicine. Preventive medicine has been largely relegated to the Public Health Service. Medical education provides minimal time and instruction in preventive medicine. Third-party insurers eschew payments for preventive interventions, as is the case with Medicare, or skimpily support secondary or tertiary preventive measures. I think any impartial examination of the evidence would indicate the need for a major change in the emphasis.[10]

A medical system's functioning most effectively at the lowest cost means the entire system acts completely in tune with the underlying order or natural laws that govern human health to avoid disease. Dr. David Greaves has noted, "Man is himself part of

> To produce an efficient medical system, the path of least action is to establish and maintain effective, comprehensive disease-prevention and health-promotion programs.

nature, and so must learn how best to accommodate it."[11] Biomedicine's reductionism, one cause one effect model, single active ingredient theory, mind-body separation, and undue reliance on physical explanations for diseases restrict the growth of the knowledge that guides the medical system. These limitations decrease the capacity of medical professionals to educate and inspire their patients to stay healthy. The shared understandings of the emerging models suggest that a new medical theory must elucidate how the human race can best live in accord with natural law to achieve balance, harmony, and integration in all areas of life (spiritual, mental, physical, social, economic, and environmental). To reform health care systems, we need a comprehensive understanding of all of the natural laws that affect human health and disease. Current medical research and education fall short and must be completely restructured to achieve this goal.

# Chapter 4

# Something Old, Something New: The Value of Scientifically Verified Complementary and Alternative Medicine (CAM)

*"Consumer demand for CAM is motivating more managed care organizations and insurance companies to assess the benefits of incorporating CAM. Outcomes studies for both conventional and CAM therapies are needed to help create a health care system based upon treatments that work, whether they are conventional, complementary, or alternative."*

—K. R. Pelletier, J. A. Astin, and W. L. Haskell [1]

The use of Complementary and Alternative Medicine (CAM) is one of the fastest-growing trends globally.[2, 3] A national survey in 2002 of 31,044 adults in the United States found that 62% of adults used some type of CAM within the past 12 months.[4] This is a big increase over the use of 34% in 1990 and 42% in 1997.[5, 6] Barnes et al. found that 75% of Americans have used at least one form of CAM at some point during their lifetime.[4] CAM is surpassing some aspects of conventional medicine.

A study conducted at Harvard Medical School shows that Americans made more visits to CAM practitioners than conventional primary care physicians in 1997.[5] There are similar increases in CAM usage worldwide.[2, 3] CAM use is also growing rapidly among conventional physicians.[2]

**4.1 U.S. Visits to CAM Practitioners Surpass Visits to Primary Care Physicians**

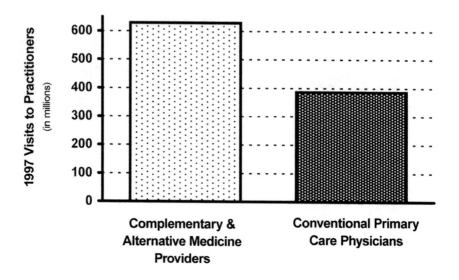

Data Source: D.M. Eisenberg et al., "Trends in Alternative Medicine Use in the United States, 1990 – 1997." *Journal of the American Medical Association* 1998; 280(18): 1569 – 1575.[7,8]

In a review of the application of CAM by mainstream medical doctors, Astin and colleagues found that "large numbers of physicians are either referring to or practicing some of the more prominent and well-known forms of CAM and that many physicians believe that these therapies are useful or efficacious."[9] In Astin's study, 43% of medical doctors referred patients for acupuncture treatment and 40% referred patients to chiropractors.[9] The most salient reasons for increased CAM usage appear to be that people "want to use all possible options in health care" and they "hope to be cured without side effects."[2]

## Complementary and Alternative Medicine Defined

The term "Complementary and Alternative Medicine" has been used in various ways. The National Center for Complementary and Alternative Medicine web site (http://nccam.nih.gov) defines CAM as "a group of health care and medical practices that are not currently an integral part of conventional medicine." A leading group of alternative medicine researchers at Harvard Medical School has defined CAM as "interventions neither taught widely in medical schools nor generally available in United States hospitals."[5] These definitions are based on CAM's interventions being unavailable in conventional medical delivery or educational systems. CAM, however, is more than an assortment of non-standard treatments; it is also a set of distinctive worldviews. CAM features entirely unique ways of conceiving of and producing health. Thus, the best way to define CAM may be to compare and contrast the shared theories, core principles, models, and worldviews among the CAM systems with those of the dominant Western medical model. In the previous chapter, we saw that CAM appears to be taking a dominant role in structuring the emerging new knowledge subsystem. In contrast, conventional biomedicine seems to be contributing very little.

## CAM Supplements Conventional Care

Eisenberg and colleagues, Astin et al., Druss and Rosenheck, and Paramore provide results from U.S. national surveys indicating that Complementary and Alternative Medicine is generally used to supplement conventional medical treatment, and not to replace it.[5, 6, 10-14] Druss and Rosenheck explained, "Unconventional therapies appear to serve more as a complement than an alternative to conventional medicine."[13] In a national survey of people who used both CAM and conventional medicine, Eisenberg and colleagues found that among their study's participants "79% perceived the combination to be superior to either one alone."[10] Astin found that 95.6% of his sample used alternative care to complement their conventional treatment, and only 4% used CAM as the sole source of primary care.[11] The same phenomenon appears to occur in Canada.[15-17] As Eisenberg and associates explained, "National survey data do not support the view that use of CAM therapy in the United States primarily reflects dissatisfaction with conventional medicine."[10]

However, they caution that CAM users are frustrated with conventional practitioners because of "their doctor's inability to understand or incorporate CAM therapy within the context of their medical management."[10] The ignorance or intolerance of some physicians is so great that most CAM users never tell their conventional doctors about their utilization of non-standard treatments. The solution may be for medical schools and Continuing Medical Education to include comprehensive courses on what CAM is and how to integrate CAM into conventional medical practice.[18] Primary care physicians would appear to be the ones best suited for this CAM integration and coordination mission. Doctors, at the very least, need to understand the non-standard health approaches their patients are using.

## The Double Standard in Medical Decision Making

Decision making in medical schools, health insurance organizations, and governments seems to be based on a double standard for evaluating conventional medicine and CAM. What is the double standard? In biomedicine, there is a general bias against CAM interventions simply because they do not "fit" with its medical paradigm and knowledge subsystem. In contrast, too frequently conventional treatments are accepted only because they "fit" with the medical paradigm and commercial interests, and not because of scientific validation. The biomedical model sometimes appears to serve as a smoke screen to hide or a justification for boosting the revenues of the Medical Industrial Complex, which seems too often lacking in concern for the safety and effectiveness of its products and services. Dr. John Abramson of Harvard Medical School may have explained why this nonscientific decision making can happen:

> The truth is that American medical practice today is based on scientific evidence as long as the evidence supports commercial interests; but all too often when the science conflicts with commercial interests, science gets nudged aside.[19]

Dr. Abramson is not alone in making this assessment. There are many other prominent doctors who have also encountered this phenomenon.[19-28] This problem of nudging science aside distorts the knowledge that guides the medical system's decision making, which may harm patient health and increase medical expenses (e.g., the Vioxx debacle). Knowledge distortion too often involves manipulating, misrepresenting, or suppressing research (See Appendix I).[19-28] As Fred Menger once quipped, "If you torture data sufficiently, it will confess to almost anything." The misrepresentation or suppression of research is often used to block the expanded use of scientifically verified CAM modalities.

**4.2 Most Conventional and CAM Methods Have Not Been Tested for Effectiveness and Safety**

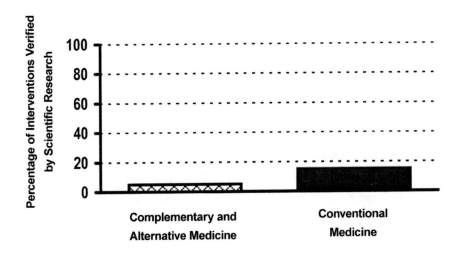

Data Sources: K.R. Pelletier "Conventional and Integrative Medicine - Evidence Based? Sorting Fact from Fiction" *Focus on Alternative and Complementary Therapies* 2003; 8(1): 3-6. R. Smith "Where is the Wisdom?...The Poverty of Medical Evidence." *British Medical Journal* 1991; 303: 798-799. J. Dalen "Conventional and Unconventional Medicine: Can They Be Integrated?" *Archives of Internal Medicine* 1998; 158:1-4.

In chart 4.2, we can see that the *percentage* of scientific evidence verifying the effectiveness and safety of conventional medicine is not much higher than that for CAM.

Biomedicine claims to be based on rigorous science, and it often asserts CAM is unproven scientifically. Yet, surprisingly, neither conventional medicine nor CAM has been adequately tested for effectiveness and safety. Of the thousands of conventional medical treatments and procedures, only 15% to 20% have been evaluated adequately by scientific research.[29-31] Over 80% of mainstream medical procedures still have not been properly or fully tested.[29-31] With rising medical expenses and concerns about the effectiveness of procedures and quality of care, most health care professionals support full testing for the efficacy and safety of these procedures. This concept is most strongly supported by adherents of Evidence-Based Medicine.

Furthermore, the *quality* of research for both CAM and conventional medicine is mixed—some is good and much is bad. In evaluating the comparative merits of scientific research on conventional and CAM procedures, Dr. Adrian Furnham of University College London explained: "The difference in the standards of evidence for orthodox and complementary therapies may not be as great as generally assumed."[2]

A double standard in medical acceptance of various healing interventions seems a disservice to patients. The ill should receive the best treatments that objective, independent science has to offer. Dr. Ronald Koretz wrote a reply to those who support the double standard in evaluating conventional medicine and CAM:

> Perhaps more importantly, we need to realize that much of what we do in our own traditional practices has no evidence of efficacy, and perhaps even evidence of inefficacy. Medical education is largely dogmatic, and we often fall into the trap of following the advice of people we perceive to be experts without actually asking them for the data. If you want to practice such an unskeptical acceptance of authority, then you should be equally unskeptical of CAM. On the other hand, if you choose to be skeptical about CAM (which, especially in the resource-limited environment in which most of us practice, is a reasonable decision), you should be equally skeptical about what your own colleagues tout and practice, especially if they ask you to do the same thing. After all, we should maintain an intellectual consistency.[32]

The requirement for the rigorous scientific evaluation of safety, efficacy, and cost-effectiveness should apply equally to both CAM and conventional procedures. Furthermore, this research should be conducted by competent organizations that do not have a direct or indirect financial interest in the procedures or products being evaluated.

## Incomplete Scientific Verification of Modern Medicine and CAM

The general public and medical professionals assume that most treatments are based on solid scientific evidence. By "solid science," we mean independent (no financial interest), rigorous experimental studies to ascertain the effectiveness and safety of the thousands of diagnostic and curative interventions in the armory of modern medicine. Surprisingly, the regulation of medical treatments is lax. They are not required to be as rigorously tested before their widespread use as pharmaceutical products by the Food and Drug Administration.[29, 30]

For instance, without adequate research before widespread application, the Coronary Artery Bypass Graft (CABG) became a standard medical treatment for hundreds of thousands of patients suffering from heart disease. The CABG is invasive, risky, and expensive. If patients fail to improve their diet and exercise habits and stop tobacco use, CABG also has questionable long-term effectiveness. In summarizing research on the value of CABG, Nortin M. Hadler, M.D., a professor of medicine and microbiology at the University of North Carolina, has explained:

> For 97 percent of the CABG patients in all three trials, there was no survival benefit from the surgery.... CABGs should have been relegated to the archives fifteen years ago, but they have not. In fact, 500,000 are still done annually in the United States.[33]

Apparently, only those angina patients with left main artery blockage benefited (3% of CABG recipients).[33] Why does the government allow hundreds of thousands of people to receive this operation when only 3% of patients who undergo CABG actually benefit from it? The Coronary Artery Bypass Graft became a standard medical treatment mainly because it fits with the "body as a machine" model. If a pipe (artery) is clogged, build another pipe around it to keep the blood flowing. This is a mechanistic approach. The CABG is also very profitable for hospitals and surgeons. Medical insurance coverage currently facilitates the proliferation of many ineffective and dangerous conventional interventions, such as CABG. It is possible, however, to unclog heart patients' arteries with non-invasive, less costly and more effective CAM interventions, which are not covered by insurance. Such interventions include dietary modifications, regular exercise, and meditation practice.[34] Isn't it mind-boggling how ineffective treatments can be widely used, while treatments that have been proved to be effective are neglected? Many people might be tempted to suspect that this phenomenon is due only to commercial interests. However, this paradox is mainly due to a lack of comprehensive knowledge. As Dr. Richard Smith, former editor of the *British Medical Journal,* has explained:

> There are perhaps 30,000 biomedical journals in the world, and they have grown steadily by 7% a year since the seventeenth century. Yet, only 15% of medical interventions are supported by solid scientific evidence. ... This is partly because only 1% of the articles in medical journals are scientifically sound and partly because many treatments have never been assessed at all.[30]

To remedy this gap, a new area of medical research and practice was developed. It is called Evidence-Based Medicine (EBM).[35] The goal of EBM is to provide the best care possible by creating clinical practice guidelines based only on the strongest scientific research. EBM uses mainly randomized clinical trials to determine the efficacy and safety of clinical procedures. This seems to be a great idea. Yet, researchers have found that physicians' "non-adherence to practice guidelines remains the major barrier to the successful practice of evidence-based medicine."[36]

Another problem is that few procedures have been evaluated by randomized clinical trials, the main EBM standard. For instance, in reviewing studies on surgical interventions, Dr. M. N. Wente and colleagues found in 2003 that "So far, only 3.4% of all publications in the leading surgical journals are randomized controlled trials."[35] While randomized clinical trials may be inappropriate for assessing many types of surgery, it is not reassuring that only 3% of these procedures have been documented by the best research as being safe and effective. Dr. Earl P. Steinberg and Dr. Bryan R. Luce have explained:

> Unfortunately, many medical practices have not been rigorously evaluated, we do not really know what their impacts on effectiveness and safety are.... More than half of all medical treatments, and perhaps as many as 85 percent, have never been validated by clinical trials. According to one expert committee of the Institute of Medicine (IOM), only about 4 percent of all services have strong strength of evidence, and more than half have very weak or no evidence.[37]

According to experts, such as Dr. J. E. Wennberg of Dartmouth Medical School and Dr. D. M. Eddy of Duke Medical Center, only 20% of our current medical and surgical procedures have been evaluated scientifically.[38] Dr. Kerr White, Retired Deputy Director for Health Sciences of the Rockefeller Foundation, has explained:

> It is still the case that only 15 percent of all contemporary clinical interventions are supported by objective evidence that they do more good than harm. On the other hand, between 40 and 60 percent of all therapeutic benefits can be attributed to a combination of the placebo and Hawthorne effects.[39]

*(The Hawthorne effect is the tendency of participants in a study to do better only due to the special attention they received.)*

Would people fly in an aircraft, if they knew it was only partially tested and verified as airworthy? Yet, according to Dr. M. Konner every day thousands of people undergo invasive and potentially dangerous procedures that have uncertain therapeutic value.[38]

This lack of scientific verification creates tremendous uncertainty in medical treatment. As Dr. K. McPherson at the University of Oxford, England has explained:

> In many situations, equally qualified physicians might disagree on which treatment is optimal. There is often no scientifically correct way to practice much of medicine. Many accepted theories concerning the treatment of illness have not been adequately assessed, and consensus based on knowledge of treatment outcomes is the exception rather than the rule.[40]

There have been a few governmental efforts to remedy this lack of research and medical uncertainty. In 1989, for instance, the United States government established the Agency for Health Research and Quality (AHRQ), formerly called the Agency for Health Care Policy and Research. The mission of the AHRQ is to evaluate medical procedures comprehensively to determine their safety and effectiveness. With a staff of approximately 300 people and a relatively small budget, AHRQ may take many decades to evaluate the thousands of untested medical interventions. Much more funding for testing is needed.

There is an emerging body of scientific research that suggests some forms of CAM are beneficial for curing sickness, preventing disease, and promoting health.[32] Other works have presented comprehensive overviews of this research. For readers who may be interested in pursuing an extensive review of the scientific research on CAM, they might want to go the web site for The National Center for Complementary and Alternative Medicine (http://nccam.nih.gov). A few examples will be presented here to give readers a general idea of what role CAM might play in improving national health and reducing medical expenses.

## Chiropractic Care

Chiropractic is a system of health care that was founded by Daniel D. Palmer in 1895 in the United States. According to chiropractic theory, misalignments of the vertebral column can affect the normal functioning of the nerves emanating from the spine that control most parts of the body. According to Dr. Palmer, mal-alignments of the vertebral column are responsible for a wide range of diseases. These disorders are remedied mainly by adjusting or manipulating the spinal column into its normal, natural position. In practice, chiropractors mainly treat patients with musculoskeletal complaints.[41] There is much demand today for chiropractic services in North America and other parts the world.

Back pain is a major reason for visits to medical doctors and a source of medical expenses, over $100 billion annually in the United States.[42] The conventional medical treatments for these disorders can often be expensive and not always effective. Biomedical therapy applies pharmaceuticals (mainly painkillers, anti-inflammatories, and muscle relaxants), surgery, and physical therapy to treat back disorders. In contrast, a major advantage of chiropractic manipulations is that drugs are not used, and thus there are no adverse medication side effects. Chiropractic care also does not use surgery, which can be risky, costly, and not always effective.

Numerous studies have compared chiropractic care with conventional medical therapies. One of the most prestigious studies was conducted at RAND by Dr. Paul G. Shekelle who concluded, "For patients with back pain, chiropractors are among the lowest-cost providers."[41] In this 1994 RAND study, the main financial savings apparently accrued because chiropractic patients were able to avoid hospitalization for their back problems.[41] In most nations, hospitalizations are usually the most costly category of medical spending.[43] By decreasing hospitalizations for back problems, substantial amounts of money were saved.

The most comprehensive evaluation of chiropractic care appears to have been made in 1993 by Dr. Pran Manga and his colleagues. They were commissioned by the Ministry of Health of the Government of Ontario, Canada to evaluate the effectiveness and cost-effectiveness of chiropractic care for treating low-back pain. After their extensive review, Dr. Manga, a health administration professor at the University of Ottawa, and colleagues concluded:

> The overwhelming body of evidence shows that chiropractic management of low-back pain is more cost effective than medical management, and that many medical therapies are of questionable validity or are clearly inadequate.... Chiropractic manipulation is safer than medical management of low-back pain.[44]

The purpose of the Manga report was to guide policy making and medical insurance coverage decisions in the Province of Ontario.

An article published in 2004 in the *Archives of Internal Medicine* reported the results of a comparison of 700,000 health plan members with chiropractic coverage with one million members of the same medical insurance plan without chiropractic coverage.[42] This four-year retrospective evaluation of health insurance claims found overall that those who used chiropractic care had lower total medical expenditures than those who did not (see chart 4.3).[42]

The back pain patients with chiropractic coverage also had significantly lower levels of x-ray and MRI usage than those without chiropractic coverage.[42] MRI utilization is usually costly. The patients with chiropractic coverage also had a lower rate of hospitalizations (40%) and lower rate of back surgeries (31%) than those without chiropractic coverage.[42] These results were all statistically significant (not due to chance). While this study was not a randomized clinical trial, its evaluation of such a large group (1,700,000 participants) forces policy makers to consider the possibility that chiropractic coverage may help improve health and reduce medical expenses.

### 4.3 Annual Total Medical Expenditures With and Without Chiropractic Care

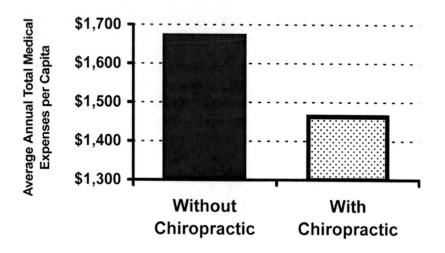

Data Source: A. P. Legorreta et al. "Comparative Analysis of Individuals with and without Chiropractic Coverage" *Archives of Internal Medicine* 2004; 164(18): 1985–1992

### 4.4 Average Hospitalizations for Back Pain Patients With and Without Chiropractic Care (per 1,000 episodes of back pain treatment)

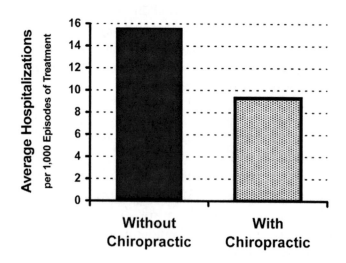

Data Source: A. P. Legorreta et al. "Comparative Analysis of Individuals with and without Chiropractic Coverage" *Archives of Internal Medicine* 2004; 164(18): 1985-1992.

ROBERT E. HERRON

Thus, when all research is considered as a whole, the weight of the evidence seems to support the use of chiropractic care to treat many lower back problems and reduce medical expenses.

## Acupuncture

In the early 1970s, acupuncture came to the United States from China. Since then, its use has increased exponentially in America and worldwide. A survey conducted in 2002 in the United States estimated that 2,136,000 people had received acupuncture treatment within the last 12 months and that approximately 8,188,000 Americans had received this treatment at some point in their lives.[4] According to the National Institutes of Health, over 10,000 certified acupuncturists were practicing in the United States, and nearly one third of these were conventional physicians who had integrated this intervention with their usual medical practice.[45]

According to the traditional Chinese perspective, the goal of acupuncture is to maintain and restore the flow of *Qi* (pronounced chee), a primal energy responsible for creating mental and physical health. When Qi is blocked, disease is generated. Acupuncturists insert thin metal needles into points on the body to restore the flow of Qi. There are approximately 2,000 acupuncture points on the human body. These points are associated with specific organs and bodily functions. In studies of the human anatomy, no scientists have ever found any physical evidence of acupuncture points, except for the seven nerve plexuses that correspond to the seven major points (also called *chakras*) in acupuncture. Furthermore, Western medical researchers have never been able to verify the existence of Qi. If Qi exists, it is at a level of the physiology of which modern medicine is completely unaware.

Nevertheless, biomedical science has found an explanation for the pain-reducing capacity of acupuncture. Researchers have discovered evidence that acupuncture points are conductors of electromagnetic signals. When stimulated by the insertion of needles into the proper points, pain-reducing chemicals produced by the body such as endorphins and opioids flow to the diseased or injured sites.[46] Research has also shown that acupuncture can change the brain's chemistry through the release of neurotransmitters and neurohormones.[47] It is worth pointing out that this biomedical research is an attempt to fit or co-opt acupuncture into the Western medical paradigm, which is foreign to the system from which it originated.

Acupuncture can also stimulate the immune system and affect involuntary processes such as blood pressure, blood flow, and body temperature. These results can be clinically useful. According to a review of the medical research by Dr. Pearl and Dr. Schillinger, this intervention is used for the following clinical purposes:[46]

- Nausea and vomiting (secondary to surgery, chemotherapy, or pregnancy)
- Pain (secondary to dental procedures)
- Addiction
- Asthma
- Carpal tunnel syndrome
- Headache
- Stroke rehabilitation.[46]

In China, acupuncture is used as sole or adjunctive therapy to treat a wide range of maladies, but in the West it is mainly used to treat pain-related disorders.[48-51] With the discovery of endorphin and opioid stimulation, Western physicians are able to *fit* acupuncture into their medical model and feel comfortable applying it in their clinical practices, even though much remains unclear about it from the biomedical perspective.

Very few researchers have attempted to assess the economic impact of acupuncture. The highest-quality evaluation appears to have been a randomized trial completed in 2002 by Dr. David Wonderling and colleagues.[52] They conducted a cost-effectiveness analysis of acupuncture to treat the chronic headaches (mainly migraine) of 401 patients in England and Wales. These participants were randomly assigned to receive either acupuncture treatments or conventional care.[52] For each quality adjusted life year (QALY) gained, they found that acupuncture costs £9180 (UK Pounds). QALY does not measure the increased total years of survival that may result from an intervention, but only the healthy years of life that are gained from it. This treatment expense compares favorably with pharmaceutical treatments for chronic headache. For instance, in the following chart there is a comparison of acupuncture and the drug Sumatriptan succinate (Imitrex), a common medication for migraine headaches. While the clinical use of acupuncture to treat headaches appears to have similar benefits of pharmacological therapy, it has the benefits of lower costs per QALY gained and fewer potentially negative side effects.[52]

4.5 The Cost-effectiveness of Treating Migraine Headaches: Comparison of the Costs per QALY Gained for Acupuncture and Usual Care Drug

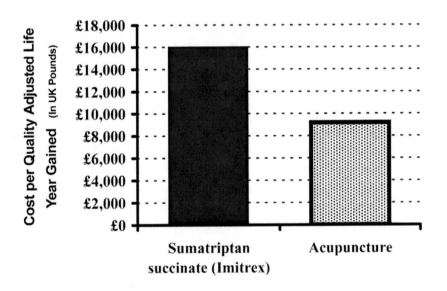

Data Sources: D. Wonderling et al. "Cost effectiveness analysis of a randomised trial of acupuncture for chronic headache in primary care. *British Medical Journal* Online, March 15, 2004; K.W. Evans et al. "Economic evaluation of oral sumatriptan compared with oral caffeine/ergotamine for migraine." *Pharmacoeconomics* 1997; 12: 565-577.

In the article "Acupuncture: Theory, Efficacy, and Practice" Dr. T. J. Kaptchuk gives another overview of the research on this ancient Chinese modality:

Numerous randomized, controlled trials and more than 25 systematic reviews and meta-analyses have evaluated the clinical efficacy of acupuncture. Evidence from these trials indicates that acupuncture is effective for emesis (vomiting) developing after surgery or chemotherapy in adults and for nausea associated with pregnancy. Good evidence exists that acupuncture is also effective for relieving dental pain. For such conditions as chronic pain, back pain, and headache, the data are equivocal or contradictory.[53]

Thus, while much research is needed to verify acupuncture's wide range of clinical effects, it merits increased research funding and consideration for application in medical systems worldwide.

## Mind-Body Medicine

Mind-body medicine appears to be one of the most widely used forms of Complementary and Alternative Medicine.[4, 54] As U.S. National Institutes of Health (NIH) researchers explained, "During the past 30 years there has been a growing scientific movement to explore the mind's capacity to affect the body. The clinical aspect of this enterprise is called mind-body medicine."[55] The NIH National Center for Complementary and Alternative Medicine has defined this term: "Mind Body Interventions employ a variety of techniques designed to facilitate the mind's capacity to affect bodily function and symptoms."[56] This CAM category includes: prayer for health reasons, biofeedback, relaxation procedures, guided imagery, numerous meditation techniques, cognitive-behavioral therapies, Jacob's Progressive Relaxation, stress management, hypnosis, Qi Gong, Tai Chi, Reiki energy healing, yoga, group support, mental healing, and many others.

Periodically, medical professionals review the scientific evidence on CAM to determine whether these procedures are efficacious, safe, and cost-effective. The NIH National Center for Complementary and Alternative Medicine maintains a web site with the latest research and recommendations for applying various CAM procedures in health care (http://nccam.nih.gov). The general consensus is that virtually every CAM modality needs better-designed research to verify its potential benefits. However, as Dr. Kenneth Pelletier has explained: "Of all the

ROBERT E. HERRON

CAM interventions, mind-body interventions in medicine are supported by the greatest body of scientific evidence for the greatest number of conditions for the largest number of people."[56] Another group of medical researchers came to a similar conclusion: "There is now considerable evidence that an array of mind-body therapies can be used as effective adjuncts to conventional medical treatment for a number of common clinical conditions."[57] Dr. John A. Astin and colleagues further explained:

> Drawing principally from systematic reviews and meta-analyses, there is considerable evidence of efficacy for several mind-body therapies in the treatment of coronary artery disease (e.g., cardiac rehabilitation), headaches, insomnia, incontinence, chronic low back pain, disease and treatment-related symptoms of cancer, and improving post-surgical outcomes.[57]

For example, 107 patients with coronary artery disease and myocardial ischemia at Duke University Medical Center were randomly assigned to a four-month training program in either exercise or stress management. After the four-month training period, participants were monitored for cardiac events for an average of 38 months. Twenty-two patients had at least one cardiac event. The stress-management group had the lower number of cardiac events, which was not due to chance (statistically significant). This study also found stress management training resulted in medical expense savings.[58]

One interesting finding on the usage of mind-body interventions is that people often failed to take advantage of those procedures for which the strongest scientific evidence documented efficacy. Dr. Peter M. Wolsko and co-researchers at Harvard Medical School further explained the under-utilization of the most effective mind-body procedures:

> While used for the full array of medical conditions, they were used infrequently for chronic pain (used by 20% of those with chronic pain) and insomnia (used by 13% of those with insomnia), conditions for which consensus panels have concluded that mind-body therapies are effective. They were also used by less than 20% of those with heart disease, headaches, back or neck pain, and cancer, conditions for which there is strong research support.[54]

This phenomenon suggests a need to better inform both medical professionals and the public so they can take maximum advantage of the most rigorously documented mind-body modalities. Dr. Gerard Bodeker of the University of Oxford Medical School and Dr. Fredi Kronenberg of the Columbia University College of Physicians and Surgeons have also suggested: "Public health research must consider social, cultural, political, and economic contexts to maximize the contribution of CAM to health care systems globally."[3]

In conclusion, for the benefit of the world's population, conventional medicine must expand its knowledge subsystem to include scientifically documented CAM procedures and models of causality. Furthermore, to reduce medical costs and protect the health of the people, all medical procedures (both CAM and conventional) should be rigorously evaluated by independent researchers with no financial interest before they are applied in widespread clinical practice and covered by insurance. For further reading on the scientific value of CAM, please see Appendix II. In the next chapter, we will examine in greater depth a form of mind-body medicine, a meditation technique that appears to improve health and reduce medical expenses.

# Chapter 5

# An Example of a CAM Method That Reduces Stress, Improves Health, and Decreases Medical Costs

*"Stress is rampant, stress is growing, and stress hurts the bottom line. A 1999 study of 46,000 workers revealed that health care costs are 147% higher for those who are stressed or depressed, independent of other health issues."*

—B. Cryer et al., *Harvard Business Review* [1]

In this chapter, we will examine a CAM intervention that eliminates chronic stress, enhances health, and reduces medical expenses. We will see that chronic stress has a powerful effect in increasing our susceptibility to disease and medical costs. Many Complementary and Alternative Medicine (CAM) modalities help to reduce stress. These methods include relaxation procedures, biofeedback, Progressive Muscle Relaxation, massage, and meditation techniques. The Transcendental Meditation technique (TM)® was chosen because it has been extensively researched and shown to reduce stress, enhance numerous aspects of health, and decrease medical expenses. We will also see how this CAM modality is related to the biomedical model.

® Transcendental Meditation and TM are registered or common law trademarks licensed to Maharishi Vedic Education Development Corporation and used under sublicense or with permission.

In a research study (see chart 5.1), Anderson and colleagues compared the impact of various health risk factors on medical expenses. They reported: "Stress was the most costly factor, with tobacco use, overweight, and lack of exercise also being linked to substantial expenditures."[2] These risk factors were statistically adjusted to be independent of all other risk categories. In the real world, high stress would contribute to most of these risk factors, but in this study each of these categories have been adjusted to show their sole, individual contribution to medical expenses without the influence of other variables. The conclusion seems to be that the prolonged exposure to excessive stress, which is inescapable in modern societies, is one of the greatest contributors to high medical expenses.

**5.1 Estimated Independent Effect of Selected Health Risk Factors on Annual Medical Costs (in 1996 U.S. Dollars)**

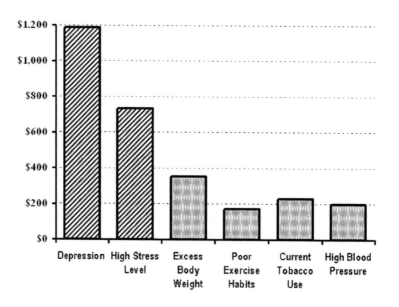

Data Source: D.R. Anderson et al. "The Relationship between Modifiable Health Risks and Group-Level Health Care Expenditures." *American Journal of Health Promotion* 2000; 15(1): 45-52.

ROBERT E. HERRON

We must understand what *stress* is and why it affects health so dramatically. There have been numerous definitions of stress in a wide range of scientific disciplines; none have been considered fully satisfactory. However, for scientific research and discussion we must have a working definition. Dr. G. Chrousos and Dr. P. Gold explained the current medical understanding of this term:

> Living organisms survive by maintaining an immensely complex dynamic and harmonious equilibrium, or homeostasis, that is constantly challenged or outright threatened by intrinsic or extrinsic disturbing forces or stressors. The steady state required for successful adaptation is maintained by counteracting/reestablishing forces, or adaptational responses, consisting of an extraordinary repertoire of physical or mental reactions that attempt to counteract the effects of the stressors in order to reestablish homeostasis. In this context, we define stress as a state of disharmony, or threatened homeostasis.[3]

Thus, stress is created when individuals experience excessive psychological and/or physical demands, and their state of homeostasis (physiological balance) is threatened.

## Chronic Stress and Health

*Stress can make us sick, and a critical shift in medicine has been the recognition that many of the damaging diseases of slow accumulation can be either caused or made far worse by stress.*

—Dr. R. M. Sapolsky[4]

Our immune system protects the body from diseases. One of the most important ways that chronic stress affects health is by degrading our immune system.[5] As the immune system is weakened, we become increasingly susceptible to a wide range of disorders.[4] Chronic stress is the excessive activation of the stress response (flight or fight). This over-activation leads to high levels of cortisol, other neuromodulators, and free radicals that weaken the immune system and increase our vulnerability to chronic and immune-related diseases, including cardiovascular disease, cancer, and many other disorders.[3, 6-8] Thus, too much stress over long periods can become a major threat to health.[3, 6-8] With the increases in stress-related diseases, medical expenses also rise.

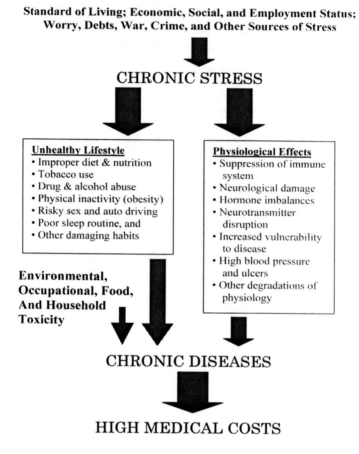

Standard of Living; Economic, Social, and Employment Status;
Worry, Debts, War, Crime, and Other Sources of Stress

CHRONIC STRESS

**Unhealthy Lifestyle**
• Improper diet & nutrition
• Tobacco use
• Drug & alcohol abuse
• Physical inactivity (obesity)
• Risky sex and auto driving
• Poor sleep routine, and
• Other damaging habits

**Physiological Effects**
• Suppression of immune system
• Neurological damage
• Hormone imbalances
• Neurotransmitter disruption
• Increased vulnerability to disease
• High blood pressure and ulcers
• Other degradations of physiology

**Environmental, Occupational, Food, And Household Toxicity**

CHRONIC DISEASES

HIGH MEDICAL COSTS

## Chronic Stress and High Medical Expenses

Approximately 75% to 80% of all medical expenses are due to chronic conditions.[9, 10] For these disorders, conventional medicine may provide some symptomatic relief, but no cure. Chronic stress can foster the development of health-damaging lifestyles, which contribute to most chronic illnesses.[11] The need to reduce stress is urgent within most nations of the world.[11] In the United States, for example, where businesses pay for the medical expenses of their employees, stress is incurring heavy financial losses. Pelletier and Lutz have explained: "Estimates of the impact of stress disorders in financial terms to businesses are that

150 billion dollars are lost annually in industrial costs due to decreased productivity, absenteeism, and disability."[12] It is estimated that 60–90% of visits to medical care professionals are for stress-related disorders.[12] In a two-year study, Tucker and Clegg found that employees with high stress were nearly twice as likely to have high medical expenses than those with less stress.[13]

A six-year study of Canadian citizens found a direct correlation between increased levels of stress and the likelihood of developing a wide range of chronic illnesses.[14] The average Canadian adult reported five sources of stress when surveyed in a large-scale study in 1994 and 1995. Dr. Shields revisited the same subjects over the years and found that each additional source of stress led to a 6% increase in the likelihood of a male's reporting a chronic illness and an 8% increase for females.[14] This epidemiological study found that chronic stress increased the odds of acquiring heart disease, arthritis, stomach or intestinal ulcers, asthma, migraines, bronchitis, and emphysema.[14] This Canadian research also suggested that undue, long-term stress is a precursor to expensive chronic diseases.[14] In another study of a major employee database, Goetzel and associates found that employees with high stress levels had 46.3% higher medical costs than their fellow employees with average stress levels.[15]

## Can We Become Stress-Proof or Stress-Resistant?

Research indicates that some CAM interventions could help us become more resilient to chronic stress. The Transcendental Meditation (TM) technique is an example. The TM technique is a standardized procedure practiced for 15 to 20 minutes twice daily while sitting comfortably with eyes closed. The practice involves the use of specific sounds that have distinctive, beneficial vibratory effects on the nervous system.[16, 17] According to scientists, the TM technique enables the mind to settle down effortlessly and spontaneously to experience more refined, quiet states of the thinking process until one transcends thinking to experience the source of thought. During the meditation session, participants report experiences of blissful pure consciousness, a state of restful alertness, a unique state of minimal mental activity with corresponding deep physiological rest and increased brain orderliness.[16-20] The founder of the Transcendental Meditation program, Maharishi Mahesh Yogi, has explained that the goal of the practice is to develop the full mental potential of the individual, which culminates in the experience of higher states of consciousness, a state of optimally developed mental and physical well-being traditionally referred to as *enlightenment*.[21] The TM program requires no belief or lifestyle change, and can be easily learned by people of any age, level of education, race, occupation, religion, or ethnicity.

The TM technique is the most basic component of a newly revived medical system. Maharishi Mahesh Yogi in collaboration with leading physicians has implemented Ayurveda according to the ancient texts. This re-enlivened system is called the Maharishi Vedic Approach to Health (MVAH), which is a comprehensive, consciousness-based system of natural medicine.[22] MVAH is prevention-oriented and has the goal of restoring balance in the physiology to maintain optimal health.[23] MVAH offers non-invasive diagnostic techniques and prescribes specific daily and seasonal behavioral and dietary routines to strengthen the immune system and the homeostatic mechanisms. MVAH makes use of an extensive *materia medica* describing the therapeutic use of medicinal plants. It includes mind-body integration strategies and techniques for reducing free radicals and strengthening the immune, cardiovascular, and digestive systems. MVAH emphasizes the role of the environment in maintaining optimal individual and social health, and thus it even includes systems of education, defense, agriculture, economics, music, architecture, administration, and city planning.[22, 23]

The TM technique is unique because its principles and practice are fundamentally different from those of other meditation and relaxation procedures.[24,25] With regard to the effects of the TM technique in diminishing stress, Dr. Hans Selye, a pioneer medical researcher of stress-related diseases, explained:

> Research already conducted shows that physiological effects of Transcendental Meditation are exactly opposite to those identified by medicine as being characteristic of the body's effort to meet the demands of stress. The TM technique is a method, which so relaxes the human central nervous system...it doesn't suffer from stress.... And I

think if you can influence the nervous system through Transcendental Meditation so that it can really relax, really be at its best in responding non-specifically to any demand, that would be an ideal solution.[26]

Since chronic stress affects health status, which is the main determinant of high-cost medical usage, we will briefly review the scientific evidence on the health-related outcomes that accrue from practice of the TM technique. Then, we will examine the possible efficacy of this technique in helping to reduce medical expenses.

## Health-Related Research

Of all meditation and relaxation techniques available today, the Transcendental Meditation program is the best-researched procedure. More than 600 research studies have documented a wide range of benefits that result from this meditation. These studies have been conducted at more than 250 universities and research institutions in over 33 countries.

Research indicates the TM technique produced enhanced happiness, optimization of brain functioning, increased intelligence, improved memory, increased creativity, improved academic performance, increased mental and physical energy, improved relationships, reduced societal tensions, and reversal of biological aging. An important side benefit is that TM practice also produces physiological and psychological effects that neutralize chronic stress.

## The Physiological Effects of the Transcendental Meditation Technique in Eliminating Stress

- Improved neuroendocrine balance and function[27-28]

- Lower baseline cortisol levels[29-32]

- Reduced respiratory rate[19, 33, 34]

- Reduced blood pressure in both normal[35-37] and hypertensive patients[38, 39]

- Decreased heart rate[19, 20, 34]

- Global reduction in somatic arousal (general measure of physiological excitation)[18]

The U.S. National Institutes of Health (NIH) has funded numerous studies that have evaluated the impact of the TM technique on cardiovascular outcomes.[23] The list below shows the research results from studies that were mainly funded by NIH.

### Summary of Cardiovascular Results

- Reduction in cardiovascular disease[40-47]

- Reduction of high blood pressure[38, 39, 48]

- Regression of atherosclerosis[46]

- Improvement in angina pectoris[47]

- Improvement in heart functioning[48, 49]

- Decreased cardiovascular mortality.[40, 41, 50]

In addition to individual research studies, there are meta-analyses that have shown that the technique is effective in several areas that can affect health status and medical expenses. Meta-analysis is a statistical method for synthesizing and comparing the results of many research studies. Dr. D.W. Orme-Johnson of Florida has performed meta-analyses that suggest there are substantial differences in the effectiveness of procedures for decreasing stress.[24] Several comparative studies have suggested that the TM technique appears to produce distinctive results in eliminating chronic and acute stress.[24, 25, 51-54] Numerous randomized clinical trials are included in the following meta-analyses.

### 5.3 Comparison of the Effectiveness of Relaxation Procedures in Reducing Trait Anxiety: Meta-analysis of 146 studies

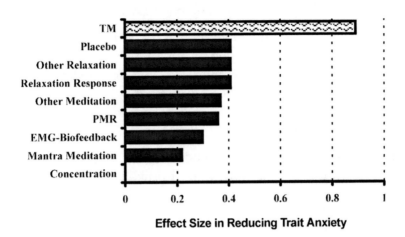

**Effect Size in Reducing Trait Anxiety**

Data Source: D.W. Orme-Johnson, K. Walton "All Approaches to Preventing or Reversing Effects of Stress Are Not the Same" *American Journal of Health Promotion* 1998; 12(5): 297-299. The Relaxation Response is the relaxation technique promoted by Dr. Herbert Benson. PMR is progressive muscle relaxation.

### 5.4 Comparison of the Effectiveness of Methods for Reducing Cigarette Use: Meta-analysis of 131 studies

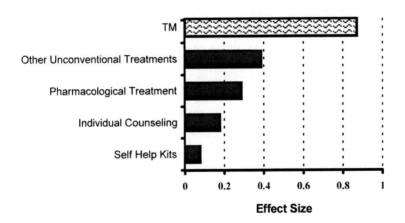

**Effect Size**

Data Source: D.W. Orme-Johnson, K. Walton "All Approaches to Preventing or Reversing Effects of Stress Are Not the Same" *American Journal of Health Promotion* 1998; 12(5): 297-299.

## Summary of Meta-Analyses of Research Showing TM Improves Health Status

### Decreased Unhealthy Habits and Lifestyle Risk Factors

Meta-analysis of 543 studies found that the TM program was more effective than other meditation and relaxation procedures in decreasing hypertension, reducing anxiety, improving psychological health, and reducing tobacco, alcohol and illegal drug use.[24]

### Decreased Substance Abuse

Meta-analysis of 198 studies found the TM program is uniquely effective for treatment and prevention of drug, alcohol, and cigarette abuse.[24, 53]

### Stress Reduction

Meta-analysis of 146 independent outcomes found the TM technique was significantly more efficacious than a placebo or other relaxation techniques in reducing anxiety (a marker of stress).[24, 25, 53]

### Deep Physiological Rest

Meta-analysis of 31 studies that compared people practicing the TM technique with people using other means to achieve deep rest found that TM produced lower respiration rate, reduced heart rate, lower plasma lactate, and higher basal skin resistance, which indicate a deeper level of physiological rest, than other methods.[24, 34]

### Increased Self-Actualization and Psychological Health

Meta-analysis of 42 treatment outcomes found the TM program was more effective than other forms of meditation and relaxation procedures in increasing self-actualization, a measure of mental and emotional well-being and overall psychological health.[24, 54]

### Reduced High Blood Pressure

Meta-analysis of 107 studies on stress reduction and elevated blood pressure that compared several popular procedures found that the TM technique was the most effective in decreasing high blood pressure, a major risk factor for cardiovascular diseases and mortality.[51]

In interpreting several research studies, Dr. Keith Wallace proposed that the brain coherence or orderliness produced during TM practice enables individuals to spontaneously develop increasingly health-supporting behaviors.[16, 17] Most of the scientific evidence supporting this notion comes from electro-encephalographic (EEG) studies. This research has found that during TM practice, the technique produces distinctive and comprehensive EEG patterns indicating enhanced brain orderliness.[16, 17, 55-58] Other studies found major improvements in health-related habits due to TM practice.[52, 53, 59-61] Dr. Lynne Mason found that this increased brain coherence grows stronger with practice over time and appears to culminate in permanent states of high level neurological orderliness that are measurable even during deep sleep.[56] Dr. Fred Travis's research found that the advanced component of the TM program (TM-Sidhi) seem to enhance this growth of neurophysiological coherence even more than the TM technique practiced alone.[62] Several neuroendocrine studies also indicate the technique generates major changes in the physiology in the direction of improved health.[27-32]

## Decreased Medical Utilization

The wide range of effects on health of this meditation would appear to also have an effect on the bottom line. Several studies suggest this procedure may reduce medical care consumption. In 1987, a cross-sectional study examined five years of health insurance data to assess the medical usage of 2,000 TM practitioners compared with controls.[63] When compared with norms (everyone else in the health insurance plan of the same age and gender) and other groups of similar profession, the TM subjects had 50% lower inpatient and outpatient medical visits. This trend held across all age groups and disease categories. Clinically significant findings included 87% less hospitalization than norms for heart disease, and 55% less hospitalization than norms for cancer.[63] This study and the following ones were completed when the TM course tuition was relatively low. Thus, there was no confounding from the wealth effect—rich people tend to have better health than people in other socioeconomic categories. The vast majority of people who have started the TM program worldwide have been from the middle class.

In 1997, an eleven-year evaluation of Blue Cross and Blue Shield of Iowa data examined the medical care usage and the economic impact of the TM technique combined with several related Maharishi Vedic Approach to Health (MVAH) interventions for health promotion.[64] These combined-modality subjects had lower medical consumption and expenditures for all age groups and in all disease categories than norms and matched control subjects of similar occupation who used only conventional medicine. For the combined modality subjects:[64]

- total medical expenditures per person were 59% lower than the norm and 57% lower than matched controls,

- hospital admissions for cardiovascular diseases were 92% lower than norms,

- cancer-related hospital admissions were 74% lower than norms, and

- mental health and substance abuse hospital admissions were 92% lower than norms.

The greatest savings were observed in TM subjects who were over 45 years old; they had 88% fewer total hospital days than matched controls. The TM program combined with the multi-modality MVAH appears more effective in enhancing health than the TM technique alone.[64]

### Decreased Medical Costs

A study conducted in Quebec, Canada by Robert E. Herron and colleagues determined whether the TM technique could help reduce the medical expenditures of people older than 65 years. After five years of practicing meditation, the cumulative average reduction in annual payments to physicians of the 163 people in the TM group relative to the matched 163 non-TM controls was 70%.[65] These results suggest the TM technique could help reduce the medical expenses of the elderly. This finding may be important because the elderly are the fastest-growing demographic category worldwide. They use disproportionately large amounts of medical care. In North America, for instance, people over age 65 comprise only 12–14% of the population, but they account for approximately one-third of all medical spending.[66-69] Government expenditures for those over age 65 are a major contributor to current and future budget deficits for which no effective solution is available.[70, 71] Does this meditation produce similar changes in younger people who tend to have lower medical expenses?

**5.5 The TM Technique Reduced Medical Expenses of People Over Age 65**

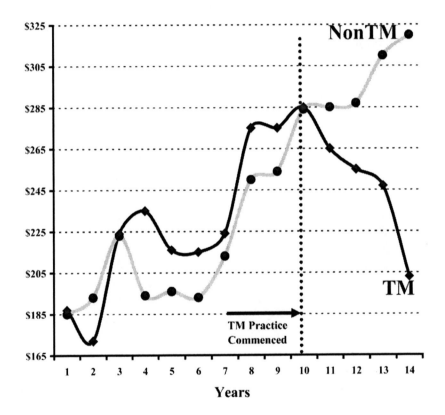

Payments to physicians for treating Non-TM and TM subjects. All participants were 65 years or older before the TM subjects commenced their meditation practice.

*Data are in constant 1992 Canadian Dollars (10% trimmed mean, inflation-adjusted)*

Data Source: R.E. Herron, K. Cavanaugh. Can the Transcendental Meditation Program Reduce the Medical Expenditures of Older People? A Longitudinal Cost Reduction Study in Canada. *Journal of Social Behavior and Personality* 2005; 17: 415–442.

Research has suggested that the TM technique also helps to decrease the medical expenses in the general population.[63, 64, 72-75] For instance, in a study published in the *American Journal of Health Promotion*, researchers compared two groups of Quebec health insurance enrollees. Both the TM and non-TM groups had an average age of 38 years. After they started the meditation, the TM group's average physician payments declined 1% to 2% annually. In contrast, the non-TM comparison group's medical payments increased up to 11.73% each year for six years. There was a 13.78% average annual difference between the TM and non-TM groups.[75] The results suggest the TM technique reduced payments to physicians between 5% and 13% annually relative to the non-TM comparison subjects over 6 years.[75]

5.6 TM Subjects Had Reduced Medical Payments Each Year for Six Years

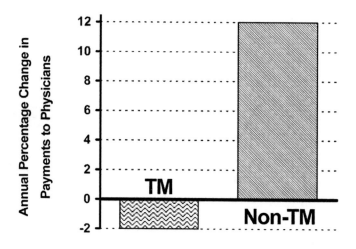

Data Source: R.E. Herron, S.L. Hillis. The Impact of the Transcendental Meditation Program on Government Payments to Physicians in Quebec: An Update. *American Journal of Health Promotion*.2000; 14(5): 284–291.

In addition, further research has indicated that the TM technique helps to reduce the fees paid to physicians for treating highest-cost patients. These individuals are the small percentage of people who consistently account for most medical expenses annually. On average, the 142 high-cost TM participants and 142 non-TM people had similar

ROBERT E. HERRON

medical expenses at the baseline when the TM practice commenced. Five years after starting meditation, the TM group's physician fees had declined by approximately 35% while the non-TM group's expenses remained higher.

5.7 The TM Technique Reduced the Payments to Physicians for Treating Consistent High-Cost People

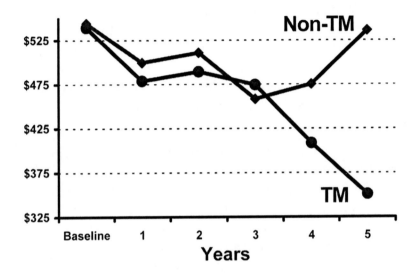

Data are in constant 1992 Canadian Dollars

Data Sources: R.E. Herron. The Impact of the Transcendental Meditation Program on the Medical Expenses of High-Cost People (*In Review*). R.E. Herron, S.L. Hillis. The Impact of the Transcendental Meditation Program on Government Payments to Physicians in Quebec: An Update. *American Journal of Health Promotion.*2000; 14(5): 284–291.

The finding that the TM technique can help decrease the medical expenses of highest-cost people is important because this procedure could be used by just a small fraction of the population to leverage large reductions in national health care expenditures. Chapter 8 has more information on high-cost people.

The most important point regarding the TM research is not the results of any single study, but the totality of all the studies, which should be evaluated as a whole. Clearly, something very important and beneficial occurs during this ancient practice that has major implications for modern medical science.

## Consciousness and Health

Briefly, we will reflect on the role of consciousness in producing human health. This will involve consideration of scientific principles that are not usually considered within the scope of medicine. The discovery that the enlivenment of consciousness (pure awareness or alertness itself) during TM practice influences health has important implications for expanding the medical model, which we examined in earlier chapters. To understand how abstract consciousness can affect the physical body, we need to know a little more about how the scientific understanding of consciousness developed.

Historically, consciousness has been thought to be a byproduct of electro-chemical interactions in the brain, which is made of physical matter. Thus, consciousness was believed to be derived from matter. Mind and matter have also been thought to be separate. Matter has become more important because it can be studied and manipulated more easily by biomedicine than the abstract and seemingly nebulous mind. Some physicists have changed this perspective. How are physics and medicine connected?

Traditionally, physics has been the leader among the sciences, because for centuries physicists have consistently unfolded the deepest and most comprehensive understandings of the physical universe. The other disciplines have been guided and influenced dramatically by the discoveries of physics. Since the development of quantum physics in the first half of the twentieth century, there have been many important discoveries that have implications for health that are currently not widely known or appreciated.

For example, the great Austrian physicist, Erwin Schrödinger (Nobel Prize for physics, 1933), proposed the existence of "one mind" or consciousness underlying all phenomena.[76] Another founder of quantum physics, Sir Arthur Eddington of the United Kingdom, explained that:

"All through the physical world runs that unknown content which must surely be the stuff of our own consciousness."[77] Sir Eddington also postulated that "mind stuff," or consciousness, is the ultimate constituent of the universe.[78]

In addition, quantum measurement theory posits that human consciousness and physical phenomena are connected at a very deep level of nature. As the French physicist Bernard D'Espagnat explained: "The doctrine that the world is made up of objects whose existence is independent of human consciousness turns out to be in conflict with quantum mechanics and with the facts established by experiment."[79] Furthermore, Dr. Max Planck (Nobel Prize for physics, 1918) asserted: "I regard consciousness as fundamental. I regard matter as derivative from consciousness."[79] Contrary to earlier beliefs, consciousness looks increasingly like the most basic component of the physical universe, from which all matter and our own physiologies are derived.[80]

This insight by Dr. Planck that matter is derived from consciousness may help to explain why the TM technique affects our physiology and health. If pure consciousness is the most fundamental level of creation from which matter is derived, then as consciousness is expanded during TM practice, it seems logical that the matter within the physiology would also be transformed. The previously reviewed research has shown that as the brain becomes more coherent during TM practice, balance, orderliness, and healthy functioning of the body are also enhanced. The research suggests a clear cause and effect relationship between the expansion of consciousness or awareness and improved physiological functioning and health. This discovery is important because it indicates that Descartes' doctrines of mind-body separation and reductionism, which guide much medical research and practice, may need to be amended. This TM phenomenon also implies that many other changes in the medical model would also be desirable. Some of these modifications are being made.

For example, Professor Tony Nader, M.D., Ph.D., is the world's leading exponent of Maharishi Vedic Approach to Health. He has developed a comprehensive model that has correlated the 40 major aspects of the Vedic Literature (i.e., the ancient science of pure consciousness from India) with each area of the human physiology.[22] He has also delineated the practical implications of his discoveries for clinical practice, disease prevention, and health promotion.[22, 81] Basically, with Maharishi's guidance, Professor Nader has re-enlivened and restored the ancient science of consciousness-based medicine that existed in India many eons ago.[22]

When we consider all of the "new" emerging health models that are converging to reshape the medical landscape, it is clear that from one angle or another, most of them recognize that there is an important connection between human consciousness and health. Modern medicine might also want to broaden its perspective and integrate the new scientific discoveries from physics and many other disciplines.[80]

# Much Needed Solutions

In Chapter 6, we will examine how expanded disease prevention and health promotion improve national health and reduce medical expenses for society.

In Chapter 7, we will show that expanded and improved primary care is essential for enhancing health and reducing medical costs.

In Chapter 8, we will see how a few high-cost people incur the majority of medical expenses annually and how caring for these high-risk people effectively could result in significant medical cost reductions.

# Chapter 6

# An Ounce of Prevention...
# Tons of Savings for Society

*"The most sophisticated and effective health care in the world cannot produce results as good as simply remaining healthy in the first place."*
—Robert G. Evans, Ph.D., University of British Columbia, Canada [1]

If a friend took you to the racetrack and invited you to bet on a horse, would you place a wager on a consistent winner or a chronic loser? Research shows that certain types of disease prevention consistently improve health and contain medical costs. As health researcher Kenneth E. Thorpe has explained "Disease prevention/health promotion approaches are key to slowing the rise in health care spending."[2] Yet, Theory Failure and commercial interests divert most funding to medical treatments that are costly, risky, and too frequently ineffective.

Theory Failure misdirects health policy and funding because the principle of reductionism guides medical researchers and clinicians to deal mainly with the smallest components of diseases, such as defective genes, molecules, and cellular imbalances. The focus is mainly on the physical causes of diseases that lead physicians to neglect the social, economic, psychological, and other non-medical aspects of health preservation and maintenance. In contrast, effective disease prevention requires that one consider the big picture—all of the components and determinants of a nation's health. This holistic view is the opposite of what most current medical education cultivates. With regard to disease prevention and national health policy, Joseph A. Califano, Jr., former U.S. Secretary of Health, Education, and Welfare, has explained:

Most important, we must change the object of our attention from sick care to health care, encourage Americans to keep themselves in far better shape and to stay out of hospitals unless they have no alternative, and give doctors incentives to keep us healthy rather than just treat us when we're ill.[3]

Several nations have improved their citizens' health and reduced medical expenses by applying disease prevention comprehensively.

**6.1 Why Not Fund Fully That Which Has the Greatest Potential to Improve Health?**

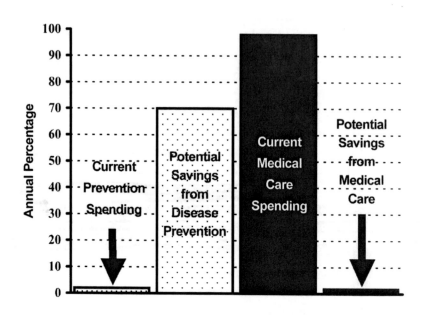

Data Sources: U.S. Dept. of Health and Human Services: *Healthy People 2010: Understanding and Improving Health*, Washington, DC: Government Printing Office, 2000. Center for Disease Control and Prevention, *An Ounce of Prevention....What are the Returns?* 2nd edition, Atlanta, GA: Dept. of Health and Human Services, 1999. *Healthy People 2000: National Health Promotion and Disease Prevention Objectives*, Washington, DC: Government Printing Office, 1990.

## The Cuban Paradox

Cuba is an example of a medical success story that was made famous by Michael Moore's documentary film *Sicko*. The paradox is that Cuba is economically isolated, technologically backward, and relatively poor. However, it has achieved national health outcomes similar to that of many developed nations, such as the United States, at much lower expense. Although America and Cuba have very different economic systems that make analyses challenging, WHO data enable surprising comparisons. For instance, these two nations have almost the same rates of infant mortality and healthy life expectancy at birth. Yet, Cuba spends only 5% of what the U.S. spends per person on health.

6.2 Comparison of Infant Death Rates in Cuba and the United States

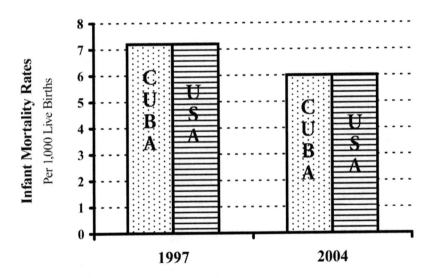

Data Source: *World Health Statistics* 2006, World Health Organization, Geneva, Switzerland.

## 6.3 Average Years of Healthy Life Expectancy at Birth (HALE) And Per Capita Expenditure on Health

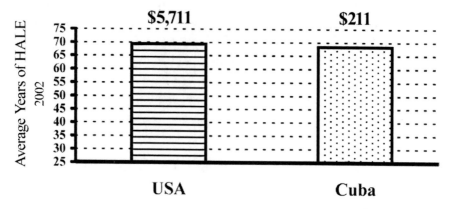

Estimated Total Per Person Expenditure on Health
(U.S. dollars)

Data Sources: *World Health Statistics* 2006, World Health Organization, Geneva, Switzerland. World Health Report: 2003, World Health Organization, Geneva, Switzerland.

Cuba appears to have one of the most cost-effective medical systems in the world. How was this feat accomplished? Spiegel and Yassi explained:

> (We) systematically examined public policy in Cuba, not only for health services but for non-medical determinants of health as well. These included education, housing, nutrition, employment, etc. plus the community mobilization and social cohesion that the Cuban system has generated. <u>It appears that the active implementation of public policy affecting a wide variety of health determinants explains the Cuban paradox, and that the international community can learn from Cuba's experience</u> (Herron's underlining).[4]

Cuba could not afford to buy an expensive, high-technology medical system like that of the United States or other wealthy nations. Instead, it focused comprehensively on the actual determinants of health, both medical and non-medical. Cuba's medical system channels most of its scarce resources toward disease prevention, health promotion, and primary care. Many capitalist nations may want to ignore the Cuban success story because of its communist system. However, economic philosophy does not determine success. For an efficient and cost-effective health care system, *what* we spend on is more important than how much we spend, or how we finance and deliver medical treatment.

Good health at an affordable cost is dependent upon spending our resources on those specific programs that produce the desired results. Each nation should systematically examine the scientific literature to identify the most effective and cost-effective preventive interventions that address the unique needs of its population. No minister of health will ever make his nation healthy by blindly imitating the so-called "advanced" nations, such as the United States, United Kingdom, Japan, or Germany. At this point in history, almost all nations allocate too much for secondary and tertiary care, and they spend too little on public health and disease prevention/health promotion.

## The Four Major Types of Medical Care

To improve health and reduce medical expenses, we need to understand the structure of medical systems. The four major categories of medical care are:

1. Public Health,
2. Primary Care,
3. Secondary Care, and
4. Tertiary Treatment (see following chart for descriptions).

All four of these general types of medical care are guided by the knowledge subsystem. These four also correspond to the course or progression of illness from the preventable, unmanifest stage of a malady, to early diagnosis and treatment by general practitioners, to later diagnosis and care by specialists, and finally to most advanced high-technology treatment by specialists and subspecialists. In looking at the following chart, we might think of these four as being connected like a stream or the flow of possibilities from public health to tertiary care.

Public health exists to prevent disease and promote health for everyone in a nation. Public health achieves its goals through various means that attempt to enhance the determinants of health, including education to facilitate proper diet and nutrition, improved lifestyles, adequate sleep, suitable exercise, obesity reduction, smoking cessation, personal hygiene, reduced substance abuse, pure water, air and food, and other improvements.

Dr. J. Bennett, an OECD researcher, has defined public health in terms of three major facets—infrastructure, intelligence, and interventions:

> Public health represents the most comprehensive bundle of policies and interventions. It describes the systematic and organised responses of society to protecting the health of its population. Public health measures are therefore diverse and include *infrastructure* support such as disease surveillance systems, workforce development of public health officers, legislation and regulation, as well as taxation and pricing policies; *intelligence* and research activities to monitor and identify emerging issues and potential health threats, as well as monitoring the patterns and trends in health status, and *interventions* aimed at protection and promotion of the health of the community, such as through organised population wide prevention or early detection services.[5]

Due to the globalization of the world's economy, bioterrorism threats, and international travel, a national public health system now must have a global focus. The reason is that even a single traveler from another nation can bring microbes into a country that could create an epidemic that could cause widespread illness and high medical expenses. The transport of the SARS virus from China to Toronto, Canada is an example of the global interconnectedness and vulnerability of health systems. Bioterrorism is a new responsibility for public health for which few nations seem adequately prepared. Typically, public health receives much less financial support, public and private, than the other three categories. The funding of public health has declined dramatically worldwide over the last two decades.[6] Yet, public health has the greatest potential to prevent disease and promote health, and thereby dramatically reduce medical treatment expenses.[7-11] We need to understand how public health is related to the other components of the medical system.

**6.4 Spending on Different Types of Medical Care in the U.S.A. (Combined Public and Private Expenditures)**

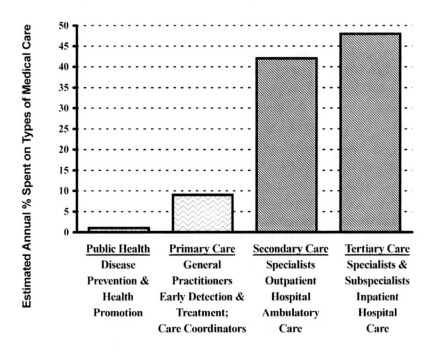

Data Sources: Center for Medicare and Medicaid Services, Health Care Financing Administration, and Statistical Abstracts of the United States; average trends over last two decades.

There are many shared functions and goals between public health and primary care, including disease prevention. Primary care is usually the first contact a person will have with a medical system. Primary care attempts to diagnose, treat, and solve medical problems in their early stages, before they become serious threats to a patient's health. Primary care is usually provided by general practitioners that also serve as medical treatment coordinators. If the general practitioners cannot solve a serious problem, they refer their patients to the best specialists available (secondary and tertiary care). When patients return from the specialists' care, the primary care doctor will usually oversee recovery and long-term disease management. General practitioners also often provide some disease prevention and health promotion interventions, if time permits. The main difference, however, is that primary care focuses on individuals and families, while public health deals mainly with the entire population. The next chapter will discuss the value of primary care more extensively.

While public health focuses mainly on populations, secondary and tertiary treatments usually focus only on the individual patients. In both secondary and tertiary care, highly paid specialists provide the most advanced high-technology diagnosis and treatment. To enter these levels of care, patients are usually referred by general practitioners. Secondary care is usually provided at outpatient clinics in hospitals or other specialty clinics, while tertiary treatment is almost always provided in inpatient acute care hospital settings. Generally, in-hospital tertiary care is the most expensive type of medical treatment. To enter tertiary care, a person usually has to be quite sick, or at risk of dying very soon if not treated quickly. In tertiary care, the hazard of medical errors is often greater than in other categories of care. The current over-reliance on tertiary care may not be the most efficient way to manage medical systems.

For three years, OECD researchers and the Health Ministers of OECD member nations comprehensively examined various ways to improve health care systems. In their report, *Towards High-Performance Health Systems*, the authors suggested:

> Ultimately, increasing efficiency may be the only way of reconciling rising demands for health care with public financing constraints.... In other words, changing how health funding is spent, rather than mere cost-cutting, is key to achieving better value.[12]

Thus, the important question is how do we increase efficiency to achieve "better value"? We have seen that the treatment-dominated medical system seems highly inefficient at enhancing population health and at reducing medical expenses. On the other hand, the potential health and economic gains through expanded disease prevention and health promotion might be great.

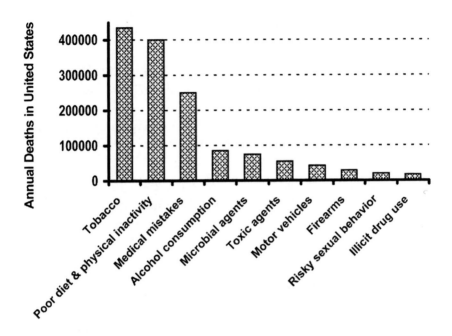

Data Sources: Mokdad, A.H., et al. "Actual Causes of Death in the United States, 2000." *Journal of the American Medical Association* 2004; 291(10): 1238-1245. Starfield B. "Is US Health Really the Best in the World?" *Journal of the American Medical Association* 2000; 284(4):483-485.

## Preventive Interventions

Some forms of public health and disease prevention appear to have substantial economic benefits and others do not. For most preventive interventions, however, we have no reliable evidence on what their cost-effectiveness might be. The research in this area has been grossly under-funded. Thus, many of the researchers who study disease prevention and health promotion have been unable to implement randomized clinical trials that are believed to provide the most accurate and reliable information with which to guide policy decisions. Nevertheless, there is an emerging body of research that suggests disease prevention and health promotion may be very cost-effective.[7-11, 13-19]

In 1994, the U.S. Public Health Service issued a report, *For a Healthy Nation: Returns on Investment in Public Health*.[8] This document outlined, in general, how various preventive interventions could help improve population health and reduce national medical expenditures. For example, the Public Health Service explained:

> Conservative estimates of the impact of population-based strategies aimed at six of the 16 areas discussed in this report—heart disease, stroke, fatal and nonfatal occupational injuries, motor vehicle-related injuries, low birth-weight, and gun shot wounds—suggest that, for these conditions alone, $68.9 billion in medical care spending could be averted between now and the year 2000.[8]

This report indicated that between 1994 and 2000, funding and implementing effectively only a few preventive methods could have saved nearly $70 billion (in 1994 dollars) and prevented millions of cases of disease and premature deaths.

In 1999, the Centers for Disease Control and Prevention published a report entitled *An Ounce of Prevention... What Are the Returns?* (2nd edition). This report was a comprehensive review of the economic impact of preventive interventions.[13, 19] The authors explained what they did:

> "This report outlines 19 strategies and demonstrates how spending money to prevent disease and injury and promote healthy lifestyles makes good economic sense. Each prevention strategy was evaluated based on the
>
> • health impact of the related disease, injury, or disability on U.S. society;
>
> • effectiveness of the prevention strategy;
>
> • costs of the disease, injury, or disability; and
>
> • cost-effectiveness of the strategy.
>
> Some childhood vaccines, for example, save up to $29 in direct medical costs for each dollar spent."[19]

As authors of the CDC report further explained: "All of the intervention strategies described for the 19 health problems presented are either cost-effective (i.e., carrying a net cost but providing reasonable value for the money invested) or are cost-saving."[13] We will briefly review several examples of cost-effective disease prevention.

## Lifestyles and Disease Prevention

Lifestyle modification can be a cost-effective form of disease prevention. For instance, Type 2 diabetes is skyrocketing in the United States and many other nations. This chronic condition is a risk factor for premature death from cardiovascular diseases and other disorders, and it is a major contributor to high medical expenses. A recent study compared the cost-effectiveness of an intensive lifestyle-modification program and Metformin, a drug for reducing high blood sugar in preventing Type 2 diabetes in adults with impaired glucose tolerance.[20] The team led by Dr. William Herman found that the lifestyle modification program was more effective and cost-effective than Metformin in preventing Type 2 diabetes in all age groups.[20] The results of this study are shown in the following table.

**6.6 Preventing Type 2 Diabetes in Adults with Impaired Glucose Tolerance: A Comparison of Lifestyle Modification versus Metformin**

|  | Lifestyle Program | Metformin |
|---|---|---|
| Delayed development of Type 2 diabetes | 11 years | 3 years |
| Reduced absolute incidence of diabetes | 20% | 8% |
| Cost per Quality Adjusted Life Year (QALY)* gained | $1,100 | $31,300 |
| Cost per Quality Adjusted Life Year (QALY) gained (from a societal perspective) | $8,800 | $29,900 |

Data Source: Herman WH, Hoerger TJ, Brandle M, et al. The cost-effectiveness of lifestyle modification or metformin in preventing Type 2 diabetes in adults with impaired glucose tolerance. *Annals of Internal Medicine.* 2005;142(5):323–332.

* Quality Adjusted Life Year (QALY) measures the healthy years of life that are gained from an intervention.

Since lifestyle modification seems to be so much more efficacious and cost-effective than drugs in preventing the onset of many chronic diseases, one wonders why medical professionals mainly rely on pharmaceutical, surgical, and related physical interventions to solve these problems.

To reduce national medical expenses, nations and provinces/states might spend at least 20% of their annual health budgets on public health—disease prevention and health promotion. The funded interventions should be verified as safe and effective through scientific research. What is the compelling logic for increasing the funding of public health? U.S. Senator Tom Harkin of Iowa has simply explained:

> In the U.S., we spend approximately $1.8 trillion a year on health care. Fully 75% of that total is accounted for by chronic diseases—things like heart disease, cancer, and diabetes—all of which, in large measure, are preventable. Meanwhile, only 2% of all health care spending is on prevention. What is wrong with this picture?[21]

This re-allocation of medical funding to provide 20% of the total health budget for public health and disease prevention would create a more balanced situation that would help improve health greatly and reduce national and state/province medical expenditures.

Overall spending on prevention has been extremely low in the United States. Only 1% - 2% of U.S. health sector funds is spent annually on primary prevention, while 98% - 99% is spent annually on various types of medical treatment.[8, 21, 22, 23] Yet, according to the U.S. Department of Health and Human Services, at least 70% of all diseases and related expenses could be avoided through the application of appropriate preventive interventions.[7, 11, 13] The majority of us were born healthy. Over time, however, mainly through our own habits and choices, we become sick. Most illness is self-inflicted.

Another example of cost-saving prevention would be tobacco-cessation programs.[24-26] Tobacco use accounts for more than 435,000 deaths each year in the United States alone and contributes to high medical expenses.[27,28] Tobacco addiction is also a global health problem. There is substantial literature delineating tobacco usage, health effects, cessation strategies, and economic impact.[26] Tobacco reduction has the potential to be a cost-effective form of prevention if conducted properly, but many of the most efficacious smoking cessation programs are also the most expensive.[24] A comprehensive multi-component approach to tobacco control would be the most effective.[10, 25]

It is highly desirable to prevent young people from acquiring tobacco addiction. However, research has shown that the quickest short-term economic benefits come from successful adult smoking cessation, especially in those with chronic conditions such as cardiovascular diseases.[26]

An additional example of a cost-effective preventive intervention would be the removal of lead-based paint from older homes throughout a nation. Lead-based paint has a sweet taste, and young children tend to eat this substance as if it were candy. This lead accumulates in their bodies. Lead is a neurotoxin that decreases intelligence and contributes to a wide range of costly health and behavior disorders in children.[29] Later, when these people become adults, their toxic accumulations also contribute to other major problems, including high crime rates. However, these diseases could easily be prevented and money could be saved from the societal perspective. In financial terms, Dr. M. L. Messonnier and colleagues found that the removing or abating of lead from a home offers a net benefit of at least $2,098. Furthermore, the abating of lead from all pre-1950 homes would yield at least $48 billion in net benefits.[13] In spite of the proven cost-effectiveness of lead abatement, these programs have received relatively little funding.

6.7 Net Amount of Medical Costs Saved by Removing Lead from Older U.S. Homes

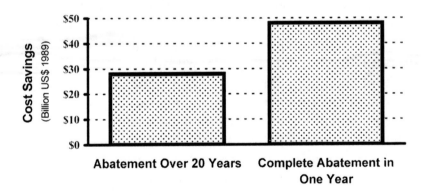

Data Source: Centers for Disease Control and Prevention. An Ounce of Prevention .... What Are the Returns? 2nd edition, rev. Atlanta, GA: US Department of Health and Human Services, CDC, 1999, page 4.

## Intelligent and Focused Health Care Funding

Our funding of disease prevention and health promotion is cost-effective from the societal perspective in the long term. In the short term, nations will have to continue to fund secondary and tertiary care adequately to care for those who currently have chronic diseases. However, there is a need to prevent high-risk people from becoming high-cost people through increased funding of disease prevention and health promotion. Investment of too much money in the wrong programs will make the crisis worse in the future.

Dr. T. M. Vogt et al. explain the need for an entirely new medical model to enable society to develop the full potential of disease prevention:[30]

> The American medical care system fails to provide effective prevention services even though some prevention services are among the most cost-effective medical procedures available. Many prevention services are routinely delivered in inefficient or ineffective ways, and new technologies may be widely and aggressively implemented despite serious doubts about their efficacy and cost-effectiveness. The barriers to effective prevention services result from conceptual limitations in our model of medical care systems, particularly the lack of a population-based perspective. A change in paradigm is needed before reforms in our health care system can improve health without bankrupting the nation.[30]

In conclusion, Cuba is an example of well-directed funding within a medical system. Other nations can also accomplish the same goals, regardless of their political systems. No political system has a monopoly on the intelligent deployment of resources. We need more effective behavior modification programs to help people adopt healthier lifestyles. We need to empower populations with self-care knowledge to enable them to maintain their health under all possible circumstances and socio-economic levels. This funding re-direction is the key to large future improvements in national health at a low cost. In contrast, increased high-technology disease treatment will yield only small gains at a high cost with many medical errors and multiple adverse medication side effects as we saw in earlier chapters. The outdated knowledge that guides the medical system must be amended or replaced for progress to occur.

Many nations, especially the United States, tend to harbor the mistaken belief that if they could only find the "perfect" financing scheme or just the right monetary incentives, all of their medical problems would be solved. This is a dangerous myth. This financial focus diverts attention from the important underlying knowledge issues, especially Medical Theory Failure. When considering that most diseases are avoidable with known preventive methods, excessive funding of secondary and tertiary care seems to be a form of *corporate welfare* to subsidize the Medical Industrial Complex. For an efficient and cost-effective health care system, *what we spend on* is more important than how much we spend, or how we finance and deliver medical treatment.

# Chapter 7

# Improve and Expand Primary Care

*"Primary care, the backbone of the nation's health care system, is at grave risk of collapse.... The consequences of failing to act will be higher costs, greater inefficiency, lower quality, more uninsured persons, and growing patient and physician dissatisfaction."*

—American College of Physicians[1]

No single solution will give us greatly improved health and reduced medical expenses. This task requires comprehensively addressing many medical and non-medical determinants of health. In this chapter, we will consider the important role of primary care in creating efficient health systems and major enhancements in population health. The full potential of primary care will only blossom within the context of an updated knowledge subsystem. We need to improve and expand primary care worldwide. In many nations, why do we see a shortage of primary care providers, especially in low-income rural and inner city areas?

Primary care doctors tend to have lower incomes, more hours of work, and more disruptions in family life than specialists. Is it surprising that too few medical students are choosing careers in this field when the need for primary care is increasing dramatically? Thomas Bodenheimer, M.D. has explained that "Between 1997 and 2005, the number of U.S. graduates entering family practice residencies dropped by 50 percent."[2]

Many reforms are needed to rescue primary care from continued decline and collapse.[2] An important one is restoring the balance in compensation between specialists and primary care doctors. Dr. Fitzhugh

Mullan of George Washington University School of Medicine framed this decline as a spiritual battle: "Many proponents of primary care have seen the primary care movement as a battle for the soul of medicine."[3] At the current time, the prince of greed seems to have stolen the "soul of medicine."

For example, a sub-specialist in Georgia told me that he worked only two days a week and spent the rest of the time dabbling in his hobbies, such as painting. Because in his geographic area there was a shortage of primary care, I asked him why he did not work as a primary care doctor in the remaining three days of the workweek. He explained that the pay was so low that it wasn't worth his time and effort. He said he could live very comfortably only working two days a week as a highly paid sub-specialist. Nearby, I knew of a middle-aged couple and others who had been looking for over two years without success for a primary care doctor. Millions of people in the U.S. have difficulties seeing a primary care physician each year. Something is out of balance. Thus far, neither governmental policy nor free markets have been able to correct this situation.

7.1 Income Comparison between Primary Care Physicians and Specialists Median Incomes in 2004 in United States

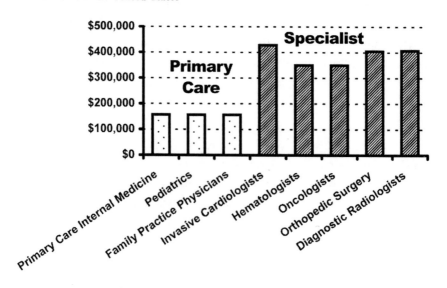

Data Source: Medical Group Management Association Physician Compensation and Production Survey, 2005.

Although specialists should continue to play an essential role in their areas, we need more general practitioners and focus on the big picture of health. Has Theory Failure helped to create the unhealthy imbalance between specialists and general practitioners? The medical model's principle of reductionism dictates that the whole can be known and controlled through mastery of the parts. Thus, the more narrowly focused a physician's training is on some small part of health, the greater his or her compensation and prestige. In contrast, primary care doctors or general practitioners are responsible for all aspects of health. Typically, specialists and sub-specialists do not think holistically. The reductionist, machine model of medicine has restricted the vision and activity of too many specialists to become *organ managers*. The outdated knowledge subsystem dictates: Fix the faulty parts and the rest will be healthy. However, excellent medicine is comprehensive. The primary care physician often serves as the only whole-patient advocate. Many people do not have a clear idea of what primary care really is or why it is so important for national health.

Primary care has been defined in many ways over the years. In 1994, the U.S. Institute of Medicine defined this profession:

> Primary care is the provision of integrated, accessible health care services by clinicians who are accountable for addressing a large majority of personal health care needs, developing a sustained partnership with patients, and practicing in the context of family and community.[4]

## 7.2 The Roles of the Primary Care Physician

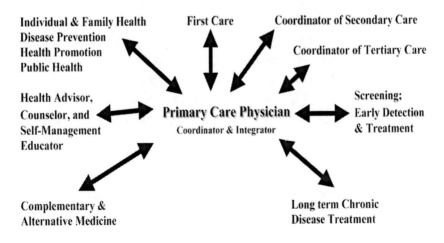

Individual & Family Health
Disease Prevention
Health Promotion
Public Health

First Care

Coordinator of Secondary Care

Coordinator of Tertiary Care

Health Advisor,
Counselor, and
Self-Management
Educator

**Primary Care Physician**
Coordinator & Integrator

Screening;
Early Detection
& Treatment

Complementary &
Alternative Medicine

Long term Chronic
Disease Treatment

Primary care (PC) is the heart of the medical treatment system. PC directly or indirectly impacts nearly every aspect of medical care. What a mother is to a family, primary care is to the medical system as a whole. The PC provider has a coordinating, integrating, nourishing, and uplifting role for maintaining both mental and physical health.

Primary care's greatest humanitarian and economic value is to serve as a platform for disease prevention and health promotion, with a special opportunity for averting disease in those who are most likely to develop debilitating and costly chronic disorders. Yet, physicians are inadequately paid by insurance organizations to provide preventive services. Through early detection and treatment, primary care doctors attempt to keep minor medical events from becoming expensive secondary or tertiary treatment episodes.

Because of their coordinating role, primary care doctors have more responsibility than specialists for ensuring that the medical system works efficiently and safely. Primary care is the central organizing power of the medical system that can make it run poorly or efficiently and cost-effectively. Dr. Robert Phillips and Dr. Barbara Starfield have explained: "The U.S. health system's failure to adopt a primary care focus results in poorer health outcomes for all Americans compared with our nation's industrialized peers, and at much greater cost."[5] They further noted in a comparative analysis of developed nations, "the United States ranked lowest in primary care functions and lowest in health care outcomes, but highest in health spending."[5]

We need to understand the complementary and interdependent roles of primary care and specialties. The primary care physician is a general practitioner who is typically trained in family medicine, general pediatrics, or general internal medicine. This physician is usually the patient's first contact with the medical system and also the one who provides coordination, continuity, and coherence of medical care and prevention. In contrast, the specialist or sub-specialist generally provides treatment for a short period of time or for a single disorder. The primary care physician needs to coordinate with the specialists to manage long-term follow-up. In some nations, such as the United States, there is often a lack of role clarity between specialists and primary care physicians. For instance, in a study of Medicare beneficiaries Dr. Barbara

Starfield and colleagues found:

> In the elderly, a high morbidity burden leads to higher use of specialist physicians, but not primary care physicians, even for patients with common diagnoses not generally considered to require specialist care. This finding calls for a better understanding of the relative roles of generalists and specialists in the US health services system.[6]

If a disorder does not require treatment by a specialist, a primary care doctor should treat it because specialists are more expensive and do not necessarily provide better care for diseases outside of their specialty. As several investigators have elaborated:

> Because specialists are more likely than generalists to suspect serious abnormalities, they are more likely to do extensive and unnecessary procedures.... Inappropriate use of specialists could contribute to explaining why costs are higher in areas with greater numbers of specialists, even though there is no improvement in outcomes among the elderly.[6]

One of the most salient roles of all primary care professionals is patient self-care education. As Dr. Thomas Bodenheimer and colleagues explained: "Under a system designed for acute rather than chronic care, patients are not adequately taught to care for their own illnesses."[7] If people with chronic diseases could be educated to assume more responsibility for their own treatment, great discomfort could be avoided and billions of dollars could be saved worldwide. Most medical spending globally (75% - 80% in U.S.) is linked to chronic conditions for which modern medicine has no cure, but only palliation (relief from some symptoms). How could primary care help improve this situation?

## Primary Care Improves Health

Research on the impact of primary care on health outcomes is a relatively new field. We need much more research. However, several scientific studies have shown that a nation's health status is directly related to the strength of its primary care system[5, 8-12] Dr. Robert L. Phillips and Dr. Barbara Starfield have explained that scientific research has shown that countries with strong primary care systems also have more effective medical systems overall.[5] They summarized the benefits resulting from strong primary care systems:

- Decreased mortality and death caused by cardiovascular and pulmonary diseases[9, 13]

- Less utilization of emergency departments and hospitals[14, 15]

- Better preventive care[16, 17]

- Better detection of breast cancer, and decreased incidence and mortality caused by colon and cervical cancer[18-20]

- Fewer tests, higher patient satisfaction, less medication use, and lower medical costs[21, 22]

- Reduced health disparities, particularly for areas with the highest income inequality, including improved vision, more complete immunization, better blood pressure control, and better oral health.[23-28]

In a study of 18 OECD nations from 1970 to 1998 that assessed the contribution of a country's primary care effort to its health outcomes, Dr. James Macinko and colleagues found that a strong primary care system in a nation reduced:

(a) all-cause mortality,

(b) all-cause premature mortality, and

(c) cause-specific premature mortality from asthma and bronchitis, emphysema and pneumonia, cardiovascular disease, and heart disease.[9]

Dr. James Macinko concluded that a comprehensive primary care system and good practice characteristics were associated with improved population health.[9] Conversely, nations with weak primary care systems experienced higher mortality rates. The shortage of primary care givers appears to contribute to poor health outcomes and high medical expenses in many nations.[8, 28] Drs. Starfield and Shi conducted research on 13 countries that examined the relationship among these variables: (a) the strength of a nation's primary care system, (b) health outcomes, and (c) medical expenses. They found: "The stronger the primary care, the lower the costs. Countries with very weak primary care infrastructures have poorer performance on major aspects of health."[10]

Expanded primary care, especially family medicine, could save many lives worldwide. Dr. Leiyu Shi and colleagues at Johns Hopkins

University evaluated the relationship from 1980 to 1995 between primary care, income inequality, and mortality rates in the 50 states in the United States. They found that greater income inequality was associated with higher all-cause death rates.[26] This was not surprising. Many other studies have documented that phenomenon. Yet, their other results were startling.

Primary care was correlated with lower all-cause mortality, and family medicine was consistently associated with decreased all-cause death rates.[26] In contrast, an overabundance of specialists was linked to increased death rates and was not related to improved population health.[26] Other studies have found similar results.[8, 29] We might suspect that the excessive deaths occurred because specialists were treating sicker people, on average, than general practitioners. However, these studies controlled for the differences in patients' health status and many other factors that could yield inaccurate results.[8, 26, 29]

7.3 In U.S. Population, on Average, Primary Care Saves Lives: All Cause Mortality Comparison Between Specialty Care and Family Medicine Primary Care

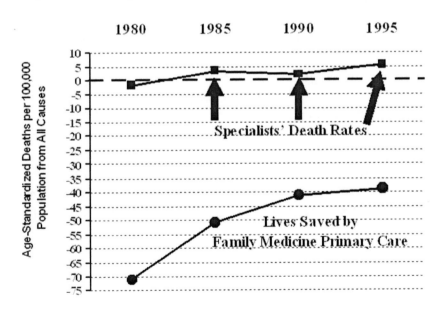

Data source for this figure: Dr. Leiyu Shi and colleagues. "The Relationship between Primary Care, Income Inequality, and Mortality in US States, 1980 – 1995." *Journal of the American Board of Family Practice* 2003; 16(5): 412 – 422.

Dr. Shi and colleagues explained: "An increase of 1 family medicine physician per 10,000 persons was associated with a decrease of 71 deaths per 100,000 in 1980 and 39 deaths per 100,000 in 1995."[26] They further suggested: "Enhancing primary care, especially family medicine, even in states with high levels of income inequality, could lead to lower all-cause mortality in those states."[26]

In an evaluation titled "The Effects of Specialist Supply on Populations' Health: Assessing the Evidence," Dr. Barbara Starfield and colleagues concluded:

> Analyses at the county level show lower mortality rates where there are more primary care physicians, but this is not the case for specialist supply. These findings confirm those of previous studies at the state and other levels. Increasing the supply of specialists will not improve the United States' position in population health relative to other industrialized countries, and it is likely to lead to greater disparities in health status and outcomes. Adverse effects from inappropriate or unnecessary specialist use may be responsible for the absence of relationship between specialist supply and mortality.[29]

The Department of Veterans Affairs (VA) maintains an extensive health care system in the United States for people who have served in the Armed Forces. In the past, the VA medical system was built around the hospital as the center of care with an emphasis on secondary and tertiary treatment. In an experiment, they reorganized some of their medical centers to increase focus on primary care. In a study that examined the effects of this reorganization, researchers found veterans who used primary care had statistically significant improvements in the continuity of care, increased rates of preventive counseling (smoking and exercise), increased patient satisfaction, decreased hospitalizations, and decreased death rates.[30] Thus, greatly increasing the supply of primary care givers, especially family medicine, is needed to enhance national health.[5, 8]

## Primary Care Reduces Medical Expenditures

*"States with more general practitioners have more efficient care and have lower spending.... Good primary care is the foundation of a good health care system."*

—Uwe E. Reinhardt, Ph.D., Professor of Economics and Public Affairs, Woodrow Wilson School, Princeton University[31]

In addition to improving national health outcomes, several studies have found that primary care can help slow the rate of increase or even reduce medical expenses.[8, 22, 32, 33] An evaluation of 22 OECD nations over a twenty-year period found that use of primary care professionals to ensure appropriate care resulted in lower national medical expenditures.[34]

In 2000, Dr. Michael F. Fleming and colleagues published a study that included a benefit-cost analysis of primary care physicians giving advice to patients to help them reduce their excessive alcohol consumption. Participants were randomly assigned into a treatment group (n = 392) that received advice on problem drinking or a control group (n = 382) that did not receive this advice. Before the study (baseline), there were no statistically significant differences between the two groups on measures of alcohol use, age, socioeconomic status, smoking, depression or anxiety, conduct disorders, drug use, motor vehicle accidents, or health care utilization.[35] After 12 months of follow-up, Dr. Fleming and colleagues reported their results:

> The total economic benefit of the brief intervention was $423,519, composed of $195,448 in savings in emergency department and hospital use and $228,071 in avoided costs of crime and motor vehicle accidents. The average (per subject) benefit was $1,151. The estimated total economic cost of the intervention was $80,210, or $205 per subject. The benefit-cost ratio was 5.6:1, or $56,263 in total benefit for every $10,000 invested.[35]

The savings observed in this randomized clinical trial are an example of what primary care doctors can do when supported properly.

Researchers at Johns Hopkins School of Public Health in Baltimore, Maryland examined the association between first-contact care, an important feature of primary care, and expenses for ambulatory care episodes in a sample obtained from the National Medical Expenditure Survey. Ambulatory care includes diagnosis, testing, treatment, preventive care, and other medical services on an outpatient basis (not in a hospital). They evaluated 20,282 treatment episodes for 24 preventive interventions and acute disease conditions. The researchers found: "Episodes that began with visits to an individual's primary care clinician, as opposed to other sources of care, were associated with reductions in expenditures of 53% overall."[22] The researchers controlled for health status, socio-demographic characteristics, case-mix, length of episode, and amount of visits to an emergency room.[22]

Dr. P. Franks and Dr. K. Fiscella, two medical researchers at the Primary Care Institute at the University of Rochester School of Medicine and Dentistry in New York, evaluated whether people using primary care doctors as their personal physician have lower medical expenses and mortality than those who choose a specialist as their personal doctor. They analyzed a nationally representative sample of 13,270 adults from the 1987 National Medical Expenditures Survey. They measured total annual medical expenses and death rates for five years. In 1998, the researchers reported their results:

> After adjustment for demographics, health insurance status, reported diagnoses, health perceptions, and smoking status, respondents reporting using a primary care physician compared with those using a specialist had 33% lower annual adjusted health care expenditures and lower adjusted mortality rates.[36]

A study in Belgium evaluated whether the continuity of care in a well-structure primary care plan provided by a family doctor had an impact on the medical expenses of individual patients. For two years, they analyzed the medical utilization patterns of 4,134 people who were divided into two groups with and without continuous care from a family physician. They controlled for a wide range of variables that were known to affect medical care use. The researchers reported: "Continuity with a family physician is related to lower total health care costs."[37]

In a study of U.S. Medicare enrollees, Dr. Peter Welch and colleagues sought to determine what factors might account for the wide geographic variation in the expenses paid for physicians' services in all

317 metropolitan statistical areas (MSAs) in the United States. Dr. Welch and his team reported: "Higher proportions of primary care physicians in an MSA were associated with a less expensive practice of medicine (i.e., lower payments for both in-hospital and out-of-hospital care)."[38] This study adds to the accumulating evidence that shows primary care doctors tend to reduce medical expenses through their less costly, more prevention-oriented, and more comprehensive style of medical practice.

In the United States, there are many examples of specific firms reducing their medical expenses by expanding and improving primary care for their employees. For instance, a large printing company in Wisconsin, Quad/Graphics, decided to spend more on primary care and prevention than it had previously allocated. This care was provided at on-site medical clinics. The result: Quad/Graphics' average medical costs per employee dropped.[39] The table below compares primary care spending, total medical expenditures, and other outcomes of Quad/Graphics with those of other local companies.

**7.4 Increased Spending on Primary Care Reduced Total Medical Expenses**

| 2003 Averages | Local Employers | Quad/Graphics |
|---|---|---|
| Primary Care expense per employee | $375 | $715 |
| Total medical expenses per employee | $7,500 | $5,500 |
| Hospital days per 1,000 employees | 298 | 170 |
| Hospital admissions per 1,000 employees | 66 | 55 |

Data Source: "One Cure for High Health Costs: In-House Clinics at Companies" by Vanessa Fuhrmans, *Wall Street Journal*, February 11, 2005, Vol. CCXLV, No. 30, pages A1, A8.

In an era of skyrocketing medical expenses, organizations may be reluctant to increase spending for anything. However, in the preceding example, increased spending on primary care and additional prevention appears to have helped reduce overall medical spending and reduce hospital admissions and the days employees spent in the hospital.[39]

## Increase Funding of Primary Care to at Least 30% of Total Health Spending Annually

*Given that conventional wisdom and good evidence indicate that a primary care physician is essential to good medical care and a primary care-based system is the ideal system, why then hasn't the United States developed one? One simple answer might be "It's the money, stupid."*

—Dr. Eric B. Larson, Dr. Kenneth B. Roberts, and Dr. Kevin Grumbach[40]

To improve national health and reduce medical expenses effectively, it is recommended that nations spend at least 30% of their total medical budget annually on primary care. Thus far, we have recommended that 20% of the medical budget be spent on public health, disease prevention, and health promotion. Now, we are suggesting that an additional 30% should be spent on primary care for a total of 50% for these most essential components of the medical system. This care should be available for all people at affordable prices. The highest priority of primary care should be disease prevention and health promotion. It is suggested that scientifically verified, cost-reducing curative procedures, disease prevention, and health promotion be targeted for the highest-risk people. Everyone, however, in a country should have access to quality primary care when they need it. Dr. Barbara Starfield has explained:

> Between 75% and 85% of people in a general population require only primary-care services within a period of a year. The remaining proportion require referral to secondary care for short-term consultation (perhaps 10-12%) or to a tertiary care specialist for unusual problems (5-10%).[41]

When we consider the actual need and where most money is spent, we see huge imbalances. Too much money is going to tertiary and secondary treatment, and too little is spent on public health and primary care. Correcting this imbalance is absolutely essential in reforming any medical system.

**7.5 Actual Percentages of Annual Usage of Types of Medical Services in U.S.**

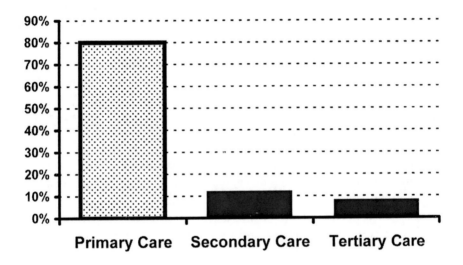

Data Source: Barbara Starfield, "Is Primary Care Essential?" *Lancet* 1994; 344: 1129 - 1133.

Many might argue that the disproportionate spending for tertiary and secondary care is justified because these types of treatment require costly equipment, drugs, and other resources and more highly trained medical professionals than primary care givers. We must always treat those who require specialists' care. On the other hand, if there were adequate public health and primary care, the need for most secondary and tertiary care would be greatly decreased in the future. In all health planning, we must keep in mind that according to extensive scientific research at least 70% of all diseases and related expenses could be avoided through the widespread application of preventive interventions.[42-44]

Dr. Barbara Starfield explained why expanded and strengthened primary care could be a good investment for any nation or organization:

> Increased attention to the importance of primary care in health services reform has resulted in studies which, for the first time, include primary care as a variable. All of them show primary care to be the most salient variable, even more important than insurance itself. That is, although financing influences access to primary care services, it is the organization of services around a primary care infrastructure that has been shown to be associated with many aspects of better health.[11]

The expansion of funding for primary care alone will not solve all of the current system's problems. There is no single, magic bullet that is going to give us improved health and reduced medical expenses. This task requires a comprehensive approach that addresses many medical and non-medical factors that determine health. In addition, the expansion of funding for primary care must occur with the guidance of an updated knowledge subsystem and improved leadership. As Dr. D. M. Berwick, M.D. and Dr. T. W. Nolan, M.D. explained:

> Science suggests that health care could, indeed, perform a great deal better than it does today and that a shared aim of improving health outcomes for patients at a cost that society can afford is sensible and within reach. However, achievement of these improvements will require of physicians not handwringing and resistance to change but concerted, positive, capable leadership.[45]

Someone needs to inspire the public to support primary care vigorously.

### Need for Leadership

To expand and improve primary care, we must find leaders from within this essential field who have the vision and courage to structure medical systems that will comprehensively address the needs of the world, especially updating the medical theory. The transition should be managed carefully. We must balance medical sector funding, keeping in mind not only economic realities, but also the cost in human suffering due to failure to effectively address preventable disorders. The transition to a better system requires leaders to be very intelligent, divinely creative, ever persistent, and extremely bold. We must remember the words of Dr. Barbara Starfield at Johns Hopkins University:

> There is no longer any doubt of the importance of primary care as the key to an effective and efficient health service....The worldwide imperative to reduce the extraordinary disparities in health across and within countries will also be served by a concerted effort to build a strong foundation of primary care services in every health care system.[28]

In spite of the essential role of primary care, it has been declining to dangerously low levels in many countries. Yet, expanded and improved primary care is <u>urgently</u> needed to increase health system effectiveness, enhance health status, and reduce medical expenses.

# Chapter 8

# An Overlooked Opportunity
# for Cutting Medical Expenses

*"It is well known that 10 percent of patients account for 70 percent of health care costs. This ratio has been strikingly stable over several decades, yet few attempts to improve efficiency have focused on improving care for the sickest patients."*

—Karen Davis, Ph.D., President of the Commonwealth Fund[1]

## The Hidden Opportunity

In this chapter, we will present a neglected opportunity for improving the efficiency and reducing the expenditures of health systems. We will also propose a strategy to take advantage of this possibility. The main point is that medical expenses are not evenly distributed. Instead, most costs are highly concentrated in three categories: people, procedures, and places.[2-6] We might consider an example of a high-cost person. One of my former professors had a mother-in-law who endured 14 heart attacks over as many years before she finally died. She had high medical expenses most years during this period. Her heart attacks also caused her considerable suffering and low quality of life.

**8.1 Percentage of Annual Total Medical Expenses Incurred by Highest-Cost 10% of People in United States**

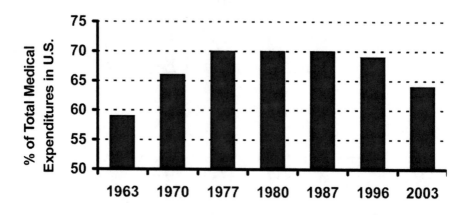

Data Sources: Berk, M.L., Monheit, A.C. "The Concentration of Health Care Expenditures, Revisited." *Health Affairs*, 2001; 20(2): 9–18. Zuvekas S.H., Cohen J.W. "Prescription Drugs and the Changing Concentration of Health Care Expenditures." *Health Affairs* 2007; 26(1): 249–257.

Why not improve how we deal with the small percentage of people who incur the highest costs, who receive highest-cost procedures, or who live in highest-cost places? These three categories might be targeted in a single coordinated campaign because they are intimately connected. These three highest-cost dimensions could be viewed as a single entity because they are ultimately different facets of the same problem — Medical Theory Failure. The current medical theory misguides and misdirects the effective deployment of medical resources. Dr. James F. Fries of Stanford University, C. Everett Koop, the former U.S. Surgeon General, and colleagues have explained: "The costs of medical care are in large part a function of the amount of illness in a population."[7] Thus, the challenge is to develop a strategy to substantially reduce the burden of disease, injury, and disability in the highest-cost people and those at risk of becoming high-cost patients in the future.

ROBERT E. HERRON

## What is a Strategy?

Before proposing a new strategy we must understand what a strategy is, because this term has been used and misused in many ways. A strategy is a comprehensive master plan stating how an organization will achieve its mission and objectives. This definition seems reasonable. However, it is incomplete. Henry Mintzberg of McGill University in Montreal, Canada further adds that a strategy is more than a plan to achieve a goal, but "strategy is *consistency* in behavior, *whether or not intended.*"[8] When an organization adopts a new plan it must also exhibit behavior consistent with that plan.

Many health-related organizations might claim to have a particular strategy, but their consistent actions sometimes indicate their real strategy is quite different. Mintzberg's observation is very important because modern medicine does not appear to have an actual "master plan" or overall strategy to achieve its mission, maintaining the health of nations. Conventional medicine, however, does have an *implied* strategy or "*consistency* in behavior." One dimension of this behavior is that it too frequently neglects the big picture of health.

In recent years, the most consistent behavior of U.S. employers who offer health insurance for their employees has been to try to reduce expenses by increasing the financial pressure on individuals and families to be more "aware" of the financial costs when they use medical services. This increased price sensitivity is created by raising co-payments for care, mandating higher insurance deductibles, offering health savings accounts, providing consumer-driven financing and delivery plans, and other means. However, these strategies have not been entirely successful. These approaches assume that all people are equally likely to incur high costs. This is not true. Consequently, these plans are unlikely to reduce medical expenses unless they are re-structured to account for the vast differences in spending patterns of highest- and lowest-cost people. The highest-cost people will consistently exceed even very high deductibles. On the other hand, the majority of people with low costs may be needlessly stressed by what they could perceive as inappropriate and even unduly harsh incentives, which will have little impact in reducing their expenses because they are already generally healthy and have very low medical costs. As currently configured most strategies will yield almost no reductions in the highest-cost people who incur most medical expenses.

## Highest-Cost People

In any population, whether a nation, province/state, city, corporation, or other organization, a small fraction of very sick people will absorb the majority of medical treatment and account for most of the medical expenses each year. The following graphs show the high-cost trends in the United States over many years.

**8.2 Percentage of Annual Total Medical Expenses Incurred by Highest-Cost 1% of People in United States**

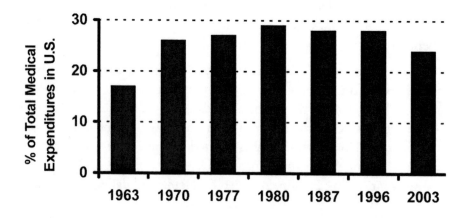

Data Sources: Berk, M.L., Monheit, A.C. "The Concentration of Health Care Expenditures, Revisited." *Health Affairs*, 2001; 20(2): 9–18. Zuvekas S.H., Cohen J.W. "Prescription Drugs and the Changing Concentration of Health Care Expenditures." *Health Affairs* 2007; 26(1): 249–257.

ROBERT E. HERRON

**8.3 Percentage of Annual Total Medical Expenses Incurred by Highest-Cost 5% of People in United States**

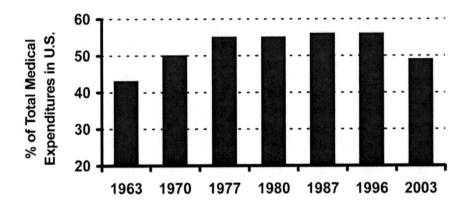

Data Sources: Berk, M.L., Monheit, A.C. "The Concentration of Health Care Expenditures, Revisited." *Health Affairs*, 2001; 20(2): 9–18. Zuvekas S.H., Cohen J.W. "Prescription Drugs and the Changing Concentration of Health Care Expenditures." *Health Affairs* 2007; 26(1): 249–257.

Some high-cost persons may have had an accident or a single episode of other injury or illness, which will increase their medical costs for only one year. Others are irregular high spenders. On the other hand, there is a special subgroup that consistently incurs very high medical expenses over time. In the short-term, individuals in this highest-cost group's spending patterns could be erratic and hard to predict, but when considering many years of data they are usually fairly consistent.

Medical researchers Berk and Monheit have published several studies on high-cost people.[2, 3, 9, 10] They have explained their results: "Five percent of the population accounts for the majority of health expenditures."[3] In contrast, the lower 50% of the population typically accounted for only 3% - 4% of total annual national medical expenses over long periods.[3] Thus, most people incur low medical expenses. These patterns have remained remarkably stable in spite of major changes in the financing and delivery of medical services. This consistent trend suggests that managed care, managed competition, etc., may have had little impact in changing high-cost patient expenses.[3]

Another study analyzed the hospital utilization of 2,238 patients whose medical records were randomly selected. It was published in the *New England Journal of Medicine* and found: "On average, the high-cost 13 percent of patients consumed as many resources as the low-cost 87 percent."[11] Dr. S. A. Garfinkel and colleagues reported, "Based on data from the National Medical Care Utilization and Expenditure Survey, the 10 percent of the non-institutionalized U.S. population that incurred the highest medical care charges was responsible for 75 percent of all incurred charges."[12]

The consistency of the high-cost case phenomenon has been documented in several other research projects.[10, 13] In a study of the persistence of high expenses over six years, Yen et al. found that the highest-cost employees (top $10^{th}$ percentile) in the starting year later incurred 80% of total medical expenses in the second year and incurred 65% of total costs during the third year.[14] Overall, the initial highest-cost employees were fairly consistent and incurred 58% of all medical expenses over the entire six-year period.[14] In an evaluation of Medicare enrollees, Lieberman et al. found the consistency of the high-cost phenomenon also holds true among the elderly (over 65 years old):

> During 1995 – 1999 the most costly 5 percent of beneficiaries in each year accounted for 47 percent of total Medicare spending, while the most costly 20 percent accounted for 84 percent of spending. By contrast, the least costly 40 percent of beneficiaries accounted for 1 percent of spending.[15]

The existence of the high-cost phenomenon has also been documented in several other studies.[16-22] Research has found that in recent years the degree of concentration has decreased a little for high-cost patients because of a slow down for inpatient treatment (hospital) spending.[23] Nevertheless, as S. H. Zuvekas and J. W. Cohen have explained, there is still a major opportunity for reducing expenses among these people:

> Even with the decline in degree of concentration, the top 1 percent of people in the expenditure distribution still account for almost one-quarter of all expenses, and the top 10 percent account for nearly two-thirds, while the half of the population at the bottom of the distribution accounts for only 3 percent of all spending.[23]

ROBERT E. HERRON

To address the needs of the highest-cost segment of the population, we must understand who they are and why their medical expenses are so elevated.

High-cost people have much more chronic illness than the general population. They tend to vacillate in and out of episodes of serious illness over several years. Health researchers K. E. Thorpe and D. H. Howard at Emory University found that most of the growth in Medicare spending was caused by people with five or more chronic conditions.[24] In other research, Dr. Paul Fishman and colleagues found that "A diagnosis of a chronic condition results in an expected increase in costs of 80 percent – 300 percent, depending on age, sex, and chronic condition profile."[25] Note this "80 percent – 300 percent" increase was observed for only one chronic disease. Consider the cost consequences of the five or more chronic conditions that are typical for high-cost people.[24] Some high-cost people inherited poor genes for health. However, most of their skyrocketing medical expenses are due to other variables, including unhealthy lifestyles, chronic stress, economic factors, psychosocial influences, and environmental toxicity.[11, 22, 26-30] In recent years, soaring obesity rates have been a major factor in increasing the prevalence of chronic conditions and their attendant costs.[31]

High-cost people are generally neither hypochondriacs nor the "worried well." The general population's main determinant of medical care utilization is *perceived* health status.[32] People go to the doctor when they perceive a need. For instance, the "worried well" may have a few extra visits to physicians and diagnostic tests each year to rule out the presence of some illness they are concerned about. For high-cost people, however, *actual health status* is the chief determinant of medical utilization.[12] Financial incentives might have little impact on these extremely sick people. If the medical expenses of the highest-cost people are to be reduced, it might be good to focus increased resources on their chronic disease treatment and address the actual determinants of their illnesses.

## Highest-Cost Conditions and Procedures

To cure disease, there are thousands of medical procedures, including a wide range of treatments and tests. Just as a small fraction of the population accounts for the majority of total medical spending annually, just a few medical conditions and their treatments account for most of the growth in health care payments. Dr. Kenneth Thorpe at Emory University and his colleagues discovered that "a small number of conditions account for most of the growth in health care spending—the top five conditions accounted for 31 percent."[4] They found that the treatment of 15 medical conditions accounted for 56% of the total change in medical care spending from 1987 to 2000.[4] Heart disease was the highest-cost medical condition to treat. Thus, of the thousands of possible medical conditions that exist, leaders could focus scarce resources on just a few disease categories, such as heart disease, to leverage large medical expense reductions.

One way to reduce the expenditures for high-cost procedures would be to eliminate unnecessary and ineffective treatments. The costs of unneeded, risky, and questionable care are too high at any price. Dr. Marcia Angell, the former Editor in Chief of the prestigious *New England Journal of Medicine* and Harvard Medical School professor, has explained:

> I suggest that a major and rapidly growing component of medical costs stems from the widespread application of tests and procedures when they are of no demonstrated benefit and may even be harmful. Identifying and curtailing such unnecessary medical care, rather than rationing beneficial technologies, should be the thrust of cost-containment efforts.[33]

Because there is extensive scientific uncertainty in medicine, unnecessary and inappropriate care can occur with surprising frequency. Dr. Thomas Bodenheimer and Dr. Alicia Fernandez have explained:

> Eliminating inappropriate care is a well-recognized strategy to reduce costs while improving quality.... Estimates of unnecessary inpatient hospital days have ranged from 25% to 50%. A recent analysis of Medicare beneficiaries 65 to 75 years of age found that 15% of coronary artery bypass surgeries were performed for an uncertain indication and 10% were inappropriate; 54% of angioplasties had an uncertain

indication and 14% were inappropriate. Increasing rates of spinal fusion surgery for conditions for which no evidence of benefit exists—with high rates of reoperation and complications—suggest substantial inappropriate care.... In 1 study, 40% of prescriptions for hypertension did not conform to evidence-based guidelines.[34]

Unnecessary surgery could be as high as 30%.[35, 36] Approximately one-third of all antibiotic prescriptions for the common flu were deemed to be unnecessary,[37] which can contribute to antibiotic resistance and the development of "super bugs," especially in hospitals. Unnecessary cesarean deliveries are rampant in some geographical areas.

How do we reduce unnecessary and ineffective care? Drs. Bodenheimer and Fernandez recommended:

> Shared decision making, in which educated and active patients are involved in treatment decisions, may be the best remedy for costly, inappropriate care. In 6 of 7 studies, shared decision making was associated with 21% to 44% reductions in more invasive surgical operations—including coronary revascularization, hysterectomy, mastectomy, back surgery, and prostatectomy—without adverse outcomes.[34]

When medicine is so vast and complex that even very intelligent medical professionals often suffer from information overload, how would we educate millions of lay patients to be informed decision makers? Updating and simplifying the medical model would help. We need a unified theory of health that both medical professionals and lay people can understand. To increase shared decision making, many physicians would have to change their current roles to include being educators and advisors. In addition, if medical professionals were organized to work together in interdisciplinary teams where they are encouraged to review each others' work and frequently consult each other on important decisions, they could reduce unnecessary testing and treatments.[38]

### Highest-Cost Places

Many researchers have observed that medical expenses can vary widely in different cities or regions of a nation.[5, 6] For instance, after qualifying for Medicare at age 65 a person will remain on Medicare for an average of 15 years. During that time, the average Medicare enrollee in Miami, Florida will incur $50,000 more in medical expenses than an enrollee in Minneapolis, Minnesota.[39] Large cities in the Northeastern U.S. and Southern California are also high-cost places. The states of Minnesota and Oregon have relatively low per capita medical expenses while South Florida, and particularly Miami, has exceptionally high costs.[40]

On the national level, we might wonder what large regional variations in medical spending really mean. Dr. Elliott S. Fisher and colleagues conducted in-depth research on this issue that was published as two major articles in the *Annals of Internal Medicine*.[5, 6] In the highest spending areas, they found that patients, on average, received 60% more medical care than patients in low spending regions. This 60% of additional services consisted of more physicians' visits (mainly in the hospital), more frequent tests, and greater utilization of specialists and inpatient care than in low-cost regions.[5] Dr. Fisher et al. explained:

> Regional differences in Medicare spending are largely explained by the more inpatient-based and specialist-oriented pattern of practice observed in high-spending regions. Neither quality of care nor access to care appear to be better for Medicare enrollees in higher-spending regions.[5]

In their second article in the *Annals of Internal Medicine*, they elaborated further: "Medicare enrollees in higher-spending regions receive more care than those in lower-spending regions but do not have better health outcomes or satisfaction with care."[6] Thus, we see again as mentioned in earlier chapters that high medical spending does not ensure better health.

A few researchers have examined whether medical cost containment should focus more on highest-cost patients or the highest-cost geographic regions to achieve maximum results.[16] Dr. S. M. Lieberman and colleagues concluded: "The evidence suggests that a focus on high-spending patients would yield the most savings to Medicare."[15] On the other hand, we must also remember that most patients' social standing, education, income, environmental toxicity, and related factors are intimately connected to their health status.

## Steps to Reduce Expenses for Highest-Cost People

Past cost-containment plans were too often directed toward the entire population and whole geography of a nation, which wasted much time, energy, and funds on a great number of people who were relatively healthy. A strategy of remedying and preventing the disorders of the sickest or highest-cost people could involve the following steps:

1. Search databases of public and private medical insurance claims to identify the high-cost cases (highest 5% or 10%). This science is highly developed: Many health insurance firms are already experts at identifying high-cost people, but they too often use this information to screen high-cost people out of medical insurance plans (adverse selection) and deny them coverage, or charge them extra high premiums.

2. Search medical records and health databases to identify those who are at risk of becoming high-cost patients (i.e., these who have multiple chronic illnesses and/or several health risk factors).

3. Research the medical literature for curative and preventive interventions that have been shown in peer-reviewed, scientific journals to heal disease, improve health, and reduce medical expenditures.

4. Offer the most cost-reducing interventions to the high-cost people and the potential future high-cost cases, including self-care knowledge.

5. Give economic incentives for people to use cost-reducing interventions that include subsidized or free treatment for the low-income groups. Give economic rewards to those who dramatically reduce their medical expenses by improving their health and risk factors for chronic illnesses. Of course, many variations of this strategy are possible.

This approach is a golden opportunity to improve health system efficiency and reduce national medical costs rapidly because it addresses the actual health problems of high-cost people.

# Summary and Action Steps

Chapters 9 and 10 consolidate the analysis and synthesis presented in previous chapters and suggest action steps for improving medical system effectiveness that enhance national health and reduce medical expenses.

# Chapter 9

# Suggestions to Reduce Medical Expenses and Improve Health

*"My view is that we are going to have to make major changes, not changes at the margins.... There's no doubt that marginal improvements in any part of the system are insufficient. We're going to need revolutionary improvements."*

—Elias Zerhouni, M.D., Director, U.S. National Institutes of Health, Bethesda, Maryland[1]

## Update or Replace the Current Medical Model and Knowledge Subsystem

The main point of this book is that the knowledge, which informs and guides a system, is the most important factor within that system. Knowledge has organizing power. If we want high quality health and low medical expenses, then we must fundamentally update or replace the current medical model. We need a knowledge system that is more accurate, reliable, and comprehensive than the current one. To guide effectively, the new knowledge subsystem would have to be fully in accord with the most advanced understandings of science, including the recent discoveries in quantum physics, self-organizing systems, chaos theory, general systems, information theory, and other leading-edge disciplines.

Governments should help promote the updating of medical knowledge through several means. They could award prizes with large financial rewards, similar to the Nobel Prizes, for advancing the development of the current paradigm through the incorporation and integration of relevant concepts from other disciplines, especially physics, traditional medical knowledge systems, and diverse cultures. In addition, governments should fund grants for conducting research and holding conferences to update the medical theory. We also need exponentially more research on public health, disease prevention, health promotion, primary care, and complementary and alternative medicine. Currently, the United States government spends less than one percent of its medical research budget in these important areas.

After a new paradigm has been developed, it should be disseminated quickly at medical schools and continuing medical education for health professionals. The new knowledge should be translated into new clinical practice guidelines. Rapidly, we need to obtain practical methods that health care professionals can apply easily on the front lines of medical practice to enhance health at an affordable price.

To ensure the support of the people in transforming national medical systems, it is important to establish the appropriate context or framework. The expansion of freedom of choice is the proper context for medical system improvement. Most people define their freedom in terms of the number of desirable choices or options they have in life. Thus, in a very open and honest manner, medical system transformation would be presented to the population as an expansion of desirable choices, not decreases or limitations for them. It is recommended that nations continue providing everything they are currently supplying. As an additional option, governments (and/or free markets where appropriate) would greatly expand and encourage choices for disease prevention, health promotion, and primary care. As people increase their use of prevention-oriented services, their health will improve. They will naturally need less high-cost secondary and tertiary care, and total medical expenditures will decline. This process may take time, but expenses will decline. The transition between the old and new systems must, however, be managed with great alertness to ensure there are no shortfalls in providing medical care to those who really need it.

In addition to updating the body of knowledge that guides the medical system, there are other recommendations for improving medical system effectiveness that will help improve health and reduce medical expenses. A series of recommendations will be proposed. Several of these recommendations are brief summaries of points in previous chapters.

## Re-Structure Medical Systems

As mentioned at the beginning of this book, W. Edwards Deming has explained, "Every system is perfectly designed to achieve the results it gets." For almost one hundred years, the medical systems of the world have been structured around the hospital. The hospital, with its great resources to provide both secondary and tertiary care, was thought to be the appropriate core for organizing most medical systems. Public health and primary care are currently on the periphery of most sickness care systems. The following table shows the structure of most medical systems, with primary care, public health, and health promotion given low priority. However, the new system would reverse these priorities.

**9.1 Proposed New Structure for Medical Systems: Re-organizing Priorities for Funding, Research, and Prestige in Medical Systems**

| Priorities | The Current System | The Proposed System |
|---|---|---|
| Highest Priority | Tertiary Care | Primary Care and Public Health (disease prevention and health promotion) |
| Medium Priority | Secondary Care | |
| Medium Priority | Primary Care | Secondary Care |
| Lowest Priority | Public Health | Tertiary Care |

This restructuring will require extensive continuing medical education for all health professionals to maximize the benefits of this new strategy.

## Reform Medical Education

Today, medical professionals need extensive knowledge in many areas, including Complementary and Alternative Medicine (CAM) interventions, which they usually do not receive in depth at medical schools. These unconventional procedures and products are used, in some form, by the majority of the world's population.[2]

Medical schools need to be in touch with the actual needs of future health care professionals. These schools should not be influenced by commercial interests, especially the biotechnology and pharmaceutical industries. Physicians' decisions determine more than 80% of all medical expenditures.[3] Therefore, they should receive the proper education to enable them to make the best decisions for their patients' health.

## Improve Unhealthy Lifestyles

If we increase funding for research to identify the most effective lifestyle improvement programs, then we can reduce medical utilization and costs by applying these interventions for the consistent high-risk persons who are most likely to become highest-cost people. For most medical professionals and their patients, the improvement of health-damaging lifestyles is extremely challenging. However, these behaviors can be changed with the appropriate interventions. We need to pay medical professionals very well for this important work. To enhance national health, the U.S. Department of Health and Human Services' report, *Healthy People 2010: Understanding and Improving Health*, recommends focusing on the following areas for improvement, most of which require major behavior change:

- Physical activity
- Overweight and obesity
- Tobacco use
- Substance abuse
- Responsible sexual behavior

- Mental health (especially depression, a stress-related disorder)
- Injury and violence
- Environmental quality
- Access to medical care.[4]

In addition to clinical duties, the best doctors are also excellent health educators and advisors to their patients. The English word "doctor" is derived from the Latin verb *docere*, which means, "to teach." As Dr. Wilfred Funk explained:

> Literally a doctor is a teacher, for his name, which is pure Latin, comes from doceo, doctus, "teach." It was originally applied to any learned man, and we have a certain survival of this when we speak of a Doctor of Letters, Philosophy, or Laws. It was not until the late Middle Ages that a doctor became more particularly a medical man.[5]

There is evidence that educating patients can reduce the need for medical care and expenses. Dr. James F. Fries of Stanford University, the former U.S. Surgeon General C. Everett Koop, and colleagues evaluated the impact of health education in reducing the need for medical care. They explained their results: "Our review of health education programs designed to reduce health risks and reduce costs identified thirty-two programs with documented effectiveness, generally achieving claims reductions of 20 percent minus the costs of the health education programs."[6] To restore effectiveness in medicine and to reduce health care costs, doctors will have to return to their original role of teaching.

### Create Global Internet Auctions for Specific Medical Procedures

As Michael E. Porter and Elizabeth Olmsted Teisberg noted in their article, "Redefining Competition in Health Care," in the June 2004 *Harvard Business Review*: "The wrong kinds of competition have made a mess of the American health care system. The right kind of competition can straighten it out."[7] To help increase the right type of competition to enhance quality, improve safety, and reduce prices, it would be valuable to establish Internet auctions, similar to eBay auctions, to sell specific medical treatments globally. Emergency medical needs require the quickest and closest treatment possible, and for these urgent cases auctions would be inappropriate. Most medical care, however, is not an emergency.

Many Americans and people in other high-cost nations are already traveling overseas to receive a wide range of less costly medical treatments. Medical tourism is one of the fastest growing industries worldwide. For instance, a friend of mine needed a hernia operation. After conducting research, he found that it was much less expensive and safer to have his operation performed in Canada than the United States, even with the extra travel costs included. The Internet medical auction could also include a wide range of prevention, diagnosis, and most other types of medical treatments. As Drs. Porter and Teisberg have explained, "The system will improve much faster if providers face competitive pressure to produce truly good results, patient by patient and condition by condition."[7]

## Pay Medical Professionals Bonuses for Improved Health

Pay medical professionals bonuses for producing the desired results—better health outcomes. There is a very simple principle in business: You get what you pay for. If we only pay medical professionals to treat disease and illness, there will always be sickness and high medical expenses. We need change. Why not pay for health? As the OECD Health Project's report explained:

> Far better would be payment methods that provide incentives to provide the right services at the right time, and that reward providers or organisations that contribute to realising performance goals, such as improved health outcomes.[8]

For this plan to work there must be accurate and reliable measurement of results and record keeping. This plan would encourage medical professionals to put more time and attention on the actual determinants of health. Since medical systems give us many things that we do not want, such as high error rates, negative medication side effects, and variable quality, why do we continue paying for them? This suggestion is also compatible with free markets, which would appeal ideologically to many leaders. Free markets usually reward those who produce the results that their consumers desire.

## Correct the Weaknesses of Health Savings Accounts

In the United States, Medical or Health Savings Accounts (HSAs) are currently thought by many to be the best way to contain rising medical expenses. HSAs are tax-free saving plans that are integrated with high-deductible medical insurance policies. HSAs transfer medical spending from employers or insurance firms to employees or individuals (self-employed). These consumer-driven arrangements do not suffer from the perverse incentives of traditional indemnity insurance in which physicians were encouraged to provide too much medical treatment that increased health care expenses unnecessarily. Dr. Martin Feldstein of Harvard University has explained: "High-deductible policies give individuals and their doctors an incentive to avoid wasteful health spending."[9] However, HSAs also have weaknesses that need to be corrected. For instance, in most HSAs, participants can spend their money only on medical treatment, and not for disease prevention or health promotion. Researchers also found: "Medical Savings Accounts will not save money but will instead, under most formulations, lead to an increase in spending on the healthiest members of the population."[10] For HSAs to succeed in containing or reducing medical expenses, the following points need to be addressed:

- All HSAs should allow spending on scientifically documented disease prevention and health promotion interventions.

- All HSAs should also allow spending on Traditional, Complementary and Alternative Medicine interventions that have been scientifically verified to be safe and medically effective.

- HSAs should be re-organized to prevent low-income people and the working poor from having to pay high deductibles they cannot afford.

- HSAs are unlikely to reduce medical expenses unless they are re-structured to account for the vast differences in spending patterns of highest and lowest-cost people (see Chapter 8). As currently configured HSAs will yield almost no reductions in the highest-cost people who incur most medical expenses.

While HSAs have great promise to help reduce medical expenses, the potential gains will be realized only if they are re-structured to address the above issues.

## Give Safety the Highest Priority in All Decisions That Affect Health

The Precautionary Principle is most simply expressed as *Safety First*. To improve health in a nation, the Precautionary Principle should be adopted as one of the country's most important values. When making decisions that directly or indirectly affect the health of their people, nations should favor caution, instead of taking unnecessary risks that might undermine the health of their citizenry and thereby increase medical expenses. Historically, many substances that have been approved for use were later found to harm health, including dichlorodiphenyltrichloroethane (DDT), polychlorinated biphenyls (PCBs), polybrominated diphenyl ethers (PBDEs), and methyl tertiary-butyl ether (MTBE). Because many chemicals can bio-magnify up the food chain and persist in the environment for long periods, the approval of potential toxicants without comprehensive, independent testing can have long-term negative health consequences. Toxicants in the world's food, water, and environment are a major hidden driver of poor health and high medical expenditures. Of course, as these toxic chemicals weaken a nation's health, its economic competitiveness and viability are also compromised in the long term.

In some nations, such as the United States, thousands of chemicals have been approved for a wide range of industrial uses or released into the environment without adequate safety evaluations. If there is even a suspicion that something might be hazardous to national health, it should not be approved for use until comprehensively tested and shown to be safe by independent research. Potentially hazardous chemicals and all other possible health threats should be considered "guilty until proven innocent" by independent research organizations, not the companies that would profit from their approval.

## In-House Medical Clinics to Improve Health and Reduce Expenses

If any organization has thousands of employees in one location, it would probably be cost effective to establish its own in-house health care department or clinic.[11] The organization would hire its own staff of medical professionals to provide all employees and their dependents free (or very low co-payment), on-site primary care, disease prevention, and health promotion. The staff would function best if it were a multidisciplinary team of medical professionals, including primary care physicians, nurse practitioners, and public health staff to implement disease prevention and health promotion interventions. Advanced secondary and tertiary care would be contracted out as needed through competitive bidding on price and quality.

In-house medical departments give companies a new opportunity to accomplish several goals that help to reduce skyrocketing medical expenses:

1. Ensure that employees receive comprehensive disease prevention and health promotion.

2. Allow frequent tests for early detection and timely effective treatment of disorders.

3. Enable complete coordination and integration of primary care, occupational health care, and all other medical treatment and health-related issues throughout the company.

4. Facilitate comprehensive disease management for chronic conditions.

5. Control drug expenses by creating their own on-site pharmacy that provides mainly generics.

6. Eliminate the "middle man" and unnecessary administrative waste caused by reliance on medical insurance organizations and outside provider organizations and networks.

7. Do an "end run" around the chaotic, fragmented, and inefficient health system to contain medical costs and improve employee health, satisfaction, and productivity.

A note of caution: Trust and integrity are essential for this plan to work effectively. It is important that the organization protect the privacy and confidentiality of individual's medical records and treatment. This point cannot be overemphasized. If even one worker were laid off because managers discovered he was a high-cost person, a tornado of employee resentment and mistrust could cripple or end this valuable opportunity.

There are many large firms that either have their own in-house medical clinics or plan to create them very soon in the United States. These firms include Perdue Farms, Sprint Corporation, Pitney Bowes Inc., Toyota's North American manufacturing division, Kohler Inc., and Miller Brewing Company.[12] In-house medical departments could also help enhance health and reduce medical expenses in many large companies worldwide.

### Organizational Cafeterias to Ensure Healthy Diet

To ensure that employees eat wholesome meals, an organization could provide on-site cafeterias. A good diet can help reduce medical expenses.[13] Balanced, nutritious diets can help prevent a wide range of costly diseases, including cardiovascular disorders, several types of cancer (e.g., colon and prostate), stroke, and diabetes.[14-20] Researchers have found that a diet that contains fruits, vegetables, fish, red grape juice, almonds, dark chocolate, and garlic would help reduce cardiovascular disease by 76%.[21] Another diet alternative would be the Mediterranean diet, which focuses on whole grains, fruits, vegetables, and olive oil. This diet has shown numerous health benefits.[14, 22, 23] A study in the *Journal of the American Medical Association* found death rates were 65% lower in elderly persons who combined the Mediterranean diet with 30 minutes of daily exercise, no tobacco use, and moderate alcohol consumption.[22] Dr. Walter C. Willet of the Harvard School of Public Health has estimated that approximately 32% of cancer cases in the United States could be avoided with proper diet.[20]

Because of the increasing levels of pesticides and other toxicants in the food supply, the organizational cafeteria might offer organic food options.[24-26] Proper diet and nutrition would be more effective if they were integrated with other lifestyle changes.[27, 28] Furthermore, if these dining facilities were pleasant, harmonious, easy to use, and inexpensive (the organization might subsidize these cafeterias), they would also help boost morale, enhance job satisfaction, and increase retention of valuable employees. If people have proper diet and nutrition, they will be healthier and have lower medical expenses.

## Organizational Exercise Programs

Because physical fitness has been associated with good health and reduced medical expenses, it would be valuable to encourage employees to exercise regularly.[27-29] Exercises might be done at the beginning of the business day for approximately half an hour on company property. Group calisthenics are already widely practiced by many organizations in numerous countries, such as Japan, and in virtually all of the Armed Forces and sports teams of the world. Only employees with a physical disability or serious ailment would be exempted from group exercises. Additionally, the firm could build a gym on its property and pay the employees to use it. Many companies worldwide already do this. In large organizations, the encouragement and support of intramural and extramural athletic team competition would also help increase physical activity and improve team spirit. This plan would not only help improve health and reduce medical expenses, it would also help enhance group cohesion and morale.

## Expand the Computerization of Medical Records and Expand Internet Medicine

If executed properly, the application of advanced information technologies, including electronic records, Internet communication, and computer-assisted decision making, could help reduce expenses, decrease physician errors, reduce negative drug side effects, improve disease management, and enhance the quality of life.[30] For instance, researchers have found that "electronic patient charts and prescription-drug databases can reduce mistakes as much as 80 percent."[31] Prescription-drug databases could monitor all of the prescriptions for individuals to flag potential problems caused by conflicting medications prescribed by different physicians. The main focus of computer-based medicine should be on monitoring prescribed medications and facilitating physician decision making.[30] It would also be very helpful to create a new knowledge subsystem around which to structure our new decision making, communication, data storage, and information management networks. Systems that are based on the current incomplete and outdated medical model may not be as helpful as many people assume.

## Provide Universal Medical Insurance

Every nation should provide full medical insurance coverage for all of their citizens. Universal coverage means that every person within a nation can receive the timely, comprehensive health care that they need through some free or easily affordable means either public or private, or some combination of both. Because disease prevention and health promotion often take many years to show results and become cost-effective, governments might specialize in providing public health and primary care. The lifetime benefits of such programs to the entire society appear to fall within the responsibility of governments. On the other hand, free markets might contribute the most to society by competing on price and quality to provide treatment for specific types of secondary and tertiary care. Because these treatment episodes are usually short and discrete, they seem appropriate for market competition, which tends to focus on short-term results and profits. In contrast, the long-term focus of most prevention would seem to make public health and primary care less suitable for free market competition. For the best health at the lowest cost, in most nations the optimal solution may be a combination of both free market and government funding and management. Furthermore, universal medical insurance should also fund complementary, alternative, and traditional care that has been shown by scientific research to be beneficial. Fully covered disease prevention would be most important.

The pragmatic rationale for this coverage is: if people have no medical insurance, they delay treatment for minor problems that later devolve into serious disorders, which are very expensive and painful to remedy. Successful treatment is usually difficult in late disease stages. Early treatment has a better chance of success and lower costs. In other words, it is cost-effective to pay for universal medical insurance coverage from the societal perspective.

## Expand Funding and Quality of Public Health

Another key element in improving our health care system is to increase funding of public health programs up to 20% of the national and provincial health budgets. The highest priorities are the dissemination of the most up-to-date knowledge and programs to avoid disease, and preserve and promote health, especially for those who have chronic conditions. The major focus would be on educational institutions (kindergarten through Ph.D.) to teach students to avoid self-inflicted chronic conditions that account for most medical expenses. Unfortunately, in the United States and many other nations children are contracting diseases that were previously seen mainly in adults. Examples of these chronic conditions in children include Type II diabetes, hypertension, heart disease, atherosclerosis, several types of cancer, morbid obesity, and other "adult" disorders. There are dozens of scientifically documented disease-prevention and health-promotion interventions that could help reduce chronic conditions. Too often these effective programs are either underfunded or completely ignored.

## Increase Funding and Improvement of Primary Care

Everyone in a nation should have access to primary care at an affordable cost. Governments might consider increasing their funding of primary care up to 30% of the national and provincial health budgets. It would be best to increase the number of primary care professionals, especially family medicine and geriatric physicians, to eliminate the shortages of general practitioners that exist worldwide. If necessary, the U.S. government's funding for the training of oversupplied specialists could be temporarily reduced until there are sufficient numbers of primary care givers. Medical school graduates would still have the option of becoming specialists if they pay for it themselves or through non-governmental scholarships. The government could provide scholarships and grants for funding the education and training of those who agree to spend their careers providing primary care in areas where they are needed most urgently, and also offer other incentives to ensure fulfillment of the population's needs. The training of physician's assistants and nurse practitioners also could be expanded to help meet the primary care needs.

## Fully Fund Scientifically Proven Complementary and Alternative Medicine

Establish full medical insurance coverage for scientifically proven traditional, complementary, and alternative medicine (CAM) interventions. The criteria for coverage could be the publication of independent research in peer-reviewed scientific journals documenting safety, medical efficacy, and expense reductions from the societal perspective.

### Reform FDA Leadership and Drug Approval Process

The drug-related loss of life and injury is also associated with large financial losses for which society pays as a whole directly or indirectly. F. R. Ernst and A. J. Grizzle described the national medical expenses generated by drug-related problems (DRPs):

> Overall, the cost of drug-related morbidity and mortality exceeded $177.4 billion in 2000. Hospital admissions accounted for nearly 70% ($121.5 billion) of total costs, followed by long-term-care admissions, which accounted for 18% ($32.8 billion). Since 1995, the costs associated with DRPs have more than doubled. Given the economic and medical burdens associated with DRPs, strategies for preventing drug-related morbidity and mortality are urgently needed.[32]

We need to reform the U.S. Food and Drug Administration (FDA) and similar agencies in many other nations. FDA reform might include:

1. prohibition from serving in the FDA of any former employee, consultant, or attorney of a firm that is regulated by the FDA;

2. all FDA employees after their leaving the FDA should be prohibited from accepting employment, consulting fees, or any other forms of direct or indirect compensation from firms that are regulated by the FDA; and

3. the amendment of the drug testing and approval process.

There are important reasons for these reforms. Traditionally, presidential appointees to high positions in the FDA have been charged with ensuring drug safety and protecting our food supply. Some of these appointees have been executives from firms that the FDA regulates.

These appointees have a conflict of interest because they often return to the same companies that employed them before their FDA appointment.

In the current FDA drug approval process, most research to verify the safety and efficacy of a new medication is conducted by or financed by the same company that will benefit financially from the production and sale of that medication. This type of research creates a tremendous conflict of interest and is an invitation for fraud and corruption (See Appendix I).[33-42] However, in some other nations the drug approval process is very different. In these countries, a pharmaceutical firm develops a new medication that it wants approved for use. Then, this drug firm pays a fee to the government. In turn, the government uses that fee to hire an independent testing company, or even several competent independent testing organizations, such as university laboratories, to evaluate the safety and efficacy of the new drug. In most cases, the pharmaceutical company is not allowed to communicate with or influence the independent testing organizations, and in fact does not even know who is testing its drug. Ideally, the testing organization would also never know whose pharmaceutical product it is evaluating. For drug approvals, governments would be most prudent if they only used the results of the independent testing organizations, not potentially biased data produced by the drug's manufacturer (e.g., Merck and Vioxx). In addition, in testing new pharmaceutical products, they should be compared not only with placebos, but also compared with existing treatments for the same disorders. If there is no independent scientific evidence that a new drug is either more effective or less costly than current medications, then it should not be approved for use in any nation. This approach will decrease medical expenses, because new drugs tend to be more expensive than older medications.

## Create Independent Government Agency to Track Medical Errors and to Monitor Drugs after FDA Approval

Because of the high levels of injury, disease, death, and expenses arising from adverse drug events, it is important to create a national system for monitoring all prescribed medications after FDA approval. An autonomous agency would track and investigate all adverse drug events and medical errors. It would also be good to track the effects of all medical procedures.

There should be a law requiring every medical professional to report all adverse drug events and medical errors with confidentiality to a government agency that is independent from the FDA. This agency would have the full authority to reverse FDA approvals without permission from any other government entity. Medical professionals need timely, reliable, and accurate feedback so they can adjust their procedures and prescriptions based on both the short-term and long-term effects of their medications, surgeries, and other procedures. In this new agency, all employees would also be prohibited from accepting employment, consulting fees, or any other form of direct or indirect compensation from the medical care industry during or after their employment in the agency. This agency should be 100% funded by the federal government, with no direct or indirect funds from the drug industry. In addition, the people appointed to lead this agency should never have worked for any firm or organization regulated by the FDA.

### Ban All TV, Radio, and Print Advertising by Drug Firms to Consumers

The former editor of the prestigious *Journal of the American Medical Association*, George L. Lundberg, M.D. has explained:

> To control runaway medical costs, I would begin by banning all direct-to-consumer medical advertising. Advertising clearly wastes precious health care dollars and, in some cases, such as in drug advertising, inappropriately pushes for utilization that promotes commerce while undermining professionalism. It also pumps up costs. In 1990, before drug ads to consumers began appearing, drug costs accounted for about 6 percent of total health care costs in the United States. Ten years later they accounted for 11 percent. Without intervention, this percentage will soon skyrocket.[43]

In 1997, the U.S. Food and Drug Administration changed its regulations to facilitate the greatly increased advertising of prescription medications by drug firms to consumers on television and radio. People see these TV ads and often go to their doctors to demand prescriptions for expensive drugs that they might not need. Doctors know that other medications may be safer and more effective. This puts the physician in a difficult position. He wants to make his patient happy and maintain their doctor-patient relationship. He also wants to keep his patient healthy and expose him or her to the least risk from medications. Too frequently, however, to preserve the doctor-patient relationship a doctor will prescribe a requested drug against his or her better judgment. For instance, Vioxx was one of the most heavily marketed drugs in history. Think of those thousands of Americans who may have demanded Vioxx, and subsequently died of a heart attack or stroke. The Vioxx and COX-2 inhibitor debacle has greatly reduced the credibility of both the FDA and the drug industry (See Appendix I). In addition, drug advertising on TV and radio drives up national medical expenses with little health benefit. If pharmaceutical firms want to advertise to medical professionals in their health-related journals, this would be appropriate because they have the education and training to evaluate these products. However, the marketing of prescription medications to the general public is potentially dangerous and should be banned as Dr. George L. Lundberg has recommended.[43]

## Ensure Fair Pharmaceutical Prices

Medication prices should be fair for both consumers and producers. However, this is not always the current reality. For example, in the United States due to laws creating artificial barriers that restrain international trade and block competitive forces, Americans generally pay the highest pharmaceutical prices in the world.[44, 45]

Drug industry representatives have explained that Americans must pay the highest prices for medications to help finance the research and development of new life-saving drugs. Is this true? Dr. Angell explained:

> First, research and development is a relatively small part of the budgets of the big drug companies—dwarfed by their vast expenditures for marketing and administration....The prices drug companies charge have little relationship to the costs of making the drugs and could be cut dramatically without coming anywhere close to threatening R&D.[37]

Why are pharmaceutical prices so high in the United States compared with other nations?

All developed nations, except the United States, have some form of governmental drug price controls. Most of these countries are capitalist, free market states. Generally newly developed medications are patented, which means the government has given the patent holder the exclusive rights to sell a specific drug. Most governments, including Canada, Japan, and European Union, insist that if they grant patent protection from competition for a drug, they also have the right to ensure a fair market price for that medication. The United States, however, does not regulate prices, and this failure also helps to create virtual pharmaceutical monopolies.

A monopoly is defined as "an industry that produces a good or service for which no close substitute exists and in which there is one supplier that is protected from competition by a barrier preventing the entry of new firms."[46] A monopoly functions without competition, and thus invites unduly high prices and too often exploitation. In contrast, vigorous and honest free market competition helps to reduce prices in the long term.[44, 47-49]

In addition, in the U.S. and some other nations, new pharmaceutical products have been developed, in part, with government financial assistance. For instance, the U.S. National Institutes of Health gives numerous grants to universities doing research for drug firms that facilitate the development and testing of new pharmaceutical and other medical products. If the citizens' tax money pays for part or all of the development of a new drug, don't they also deserve a fair price for that medication? To reduce national medical expenses, the United States and other nations would establish strong, independent government agencies to ensure fair and just drug prices for all of their citizens.


## Repeal the Bayh-Dole Act in the U.S.

To update the knowledge subsystem and reduce medical expenses, it would be best to repeal the Bayh-Dole Act of 1980. The original intent of this law was good. The Bayh-Dole Act was supposed to improve the competitiveness of American corporations. This law facilitated the transfer of research in academic institutions that was financed by tax-payers' money into commercial products in the international marketplace. This process is commonly called *technology transfer*. However, this well-intentioned law has had many negative side effects. As university-based research became commercialized, the ethos of academia was corrupted.[37] Medical schools and researchers lost their focus and mission. Instead of being the main source of unbiased, high-quality health knowledge, under Bayh-Dole, they have become business partners of the Medical Industrial Complex (mainly drug and biotechnology firms). Academic researchers became more interested in making quick profits than conducting good science. Research projects without an obvious commercial application tended to be discouraged or ignored. For instance, the amendment of Medical Theory Failure did not offer immediate cash rewards, so it was neglected.

The Bayh-Dole Act also decreases the likelihood of serendipitous discoveries. We must remember that many medical breakthroughs were accidents. The discoveries of penicillin and the x-ray machine are famous examples. Unexpected discoveries occurred because researchers were empowered and financed to follow their curiosity and research interests, whether profitable or not. Thus, the Bayh-Dole Act has contributed to a significant decline in the quality of American medical school research and even in drug industry research and development. If the United States is going to reduce its medical expenditures, it would have to update its knowledge subsystem and scientifically verify thousands of untested medical procedures. This will never happen in the current academic milieu. When all things are considered, the Bayh-Dole Act has hurt the U.S. economy and medical system in the long term.

### Bring Real Freedom and Honesty to "Free" Markets

Governments should be careful about implementing "free market" solutions for the health sector.[47] Many people and organizations worldwide would argue that free market competition could remedy most of society's problems, including improving the medical system's efficiency and cost-effectiveness. In this view, government intervention is restricted and limited mainly to the role of a referee who ensures that all competitors are playing fairly. This free market approach has worked well in many other areas. On the other hand, in the United States and many other nations, history shows that free markets have not contained or reduced high medical expenses in the long term in spite of tremendous efforts, including managed care and managed competition.[47] Why has this failure occurred? As was explained in earlier chapters, the dysfunctional knowledge subsystem, Medical Theory Failure, and commercial interests have contributed to this dismal performance. Neither free markets nor governments have dealt adequately with these contributing factors. Why? There is inherent weakness built into many governments today.

There is quite a bit of evidence that corporations have taken over many of the functions and powers that once belonged to governments.[50-53] For instance, governments used to remove unsafe medications from the marketplace. However, a large drug manufacturer, Merck, withdrew Vioxx from the market because research showed that it caused major cardiovascular problems, including thousands of deaths. Why didn't the FDA demand the withdrawal of this dangerous medication? Have pharmaceutical firms taken over the FDA's job? Through large campaign donations, lobbying, and other means, huge multinational corporations wield undue influence on governments worldwide, especially those agencies that regulate the Medical Industrial Complex.[33-42, 50-53] The referee has been bribed. Thus, too many "free" markets have become neither free nor effective.

Too frequently, elected leaders have allowed large firms to violate laws. For the sake of boosting profits, global corporations were allowed to poison and spoil the world's health. Some pollute the air, water, soil, and food supply of many countries. This degrades health. Employers have exposed their own workers to hazardous conditions and toxicants. For the sake of short-term economic growth, many governments have even facilitated the economic exploitation (e.g., allowed extremely low wages, dangerous work conditions, few benefits) and increased the sickness of their own people.

Another problem that needs to be solved is the exponentially growing income disparities that are rampant in the United States and worldwide. This phenomenon seems to negatively impact population health. If expanding income inequality were due to vastly superior creativity and intelligence, it might have been justifiable. Yet, sadly this global trend seems too frequently due to fraud, deception, corruption, and greed. Most government leaders need to re-think their priorities and decide whether they are truly benefactors of their people, like good parents, or the slaves of dishonest commercial interests.

The expanded application of scientifically documented disease prevention, health promotion, public health, and primary care are urgently needed to enhance health and reduce medical expenses. However, without a major change in the role of governments, these improvements are unlikely to occur soon.

## Amend Nations' Organizing Principles

*"I see in the near future a crisis approaching that unnerves me and causes me to tremble for the safety of my country.... Corporations have been enthroned and an era of corruption in high places will follow, and the money of the country will endeavor to prolong its reign by working upon the prejudices of the people until all wealth is aggregated in a few hands and the Republic is destroyed. I feel at this moment more anxiety for the safety of my country than ever before, even in the midst of war."*

—Abraham Lincoln, 16th President of the United States of America

Most nations are organized around principles that explicitly or implicitly guide decision making at all levels throughout the country. These fundamental doctrines are the silent motivating force behind governments. On the surface, most societies are based on idealistic principles such as freedom, equality, justice, and human rights for all. These ideals would help enhance health. Today, however, there is a huge gap between the ideal and the real, between the talk and the action. In actual practice, the dominant organizing principle of most nations is the profit maximization of the world's largest multinational corporations. This organizing principle can affect national health and medical expenses in positive or negative ways. Today, the negative dominates.

Yet, big companies can do great things. They provide jobs for millions of people and make many wholesome, life-enhancing products.

Multinational corporations can play a major role in expanding the world's economies, providing new opportunities, raising the standards of living, and improving the well being of millions of people. It is highly laudable for corporations to earn profits through honest and fair methods that harm no one. In recent years, however, the dark side of corporate power has ascended to eclipse its great potential to help humanity. Corporations have social responsibilities. They should not work only for their own profits at the expense of everyone else's health. Governments need to ensure that corporations do not harm the health of their people.

# Chapter 10

# The Health Care System Transformation

*"If we are serious about getting control of health care costs and health insurance premiums, then we must give people access to preventive care. And we must give people the tools they need to stay healthy and stay out of the hospital."*

—Tom Harkin, United States Senate (Dem. - Iowa)[1]

Our outdated medical systems have too long neglected efficacious and cost-effective disease prevention, health promotion, public health, and primary care. We also need to more effectively address the numerous non-medical determinates of health, such as socioeconomic status and education. These omissions have cost us more in lives lost unnecessarily, more needless suffering, and more wasted expenditures than all wars and other disasters combined. In the United States, the nation with the most advanced, high-technology medical system, more than one million lives could be saved each year by applying disease prevention strategies more widely and effectively. The bottom line is not saving money, but saving humanity. Each human's health has infinite value. We must do what is right because it is our duty and highest purpose from the most profound humanitarian and spiritual perspectives.

This book has analyzed the current medical system and evaluated various innovative health care approaches. Health and happiness are not an accident. Excellent health and long life without chronic conditions and disabilities require comprehensive knowledge and total commitment. Our health leaders should provide the self-care knowledge that can help set us free from dependence on the medical system and commercial interests. Only a new seed can yield a new crop. Only new knowledge can liberate our world from the ignorance that overshadows our medical systems and societies. The inertia and resistance to wholesome change is great. However, we can find inspiration in a verse from the ancient Vedic literature of India: *Satyam Eva Jayate*—Truth Alone Triumphs. Truth in health care will eventually be victorious.

Today is the dawn. Soon, our medical systems will change radically. The domination of the fragmented parts of medical knowledge over the whole of knowledge will crumble. The medical fashions of today will become history. Instead, comprehensive education on how to act in accord with natural law will become the basis of both disease prevention and treatment. The use of drugs, radiation, surgery, etc., will decline. The use of effective alternative remedies will proliferate. Prevention will become the heart of all medical systems. Politicians will make health policy decisions based on a complete understanding of advanced medical science and the actual health needs of their people. These leaders will soon be free from the influence of commercial interests. Physicians will cease to be prisoners of their narrow and outdated education. In this new era, medical professionals will gain comprehensive knowledge to ensure the best health for the entire population at a low cost. Patients will be empowered with self-care knowledge to maintain their own health, and thus will be better able to develop their full potential in every area of life. Most of us were born healthy, but our own behaviors and environments have created most of our mental and physical disorders.

As mentioned at the beginning of this book, Jefferson has said, "Without health, there is no happiness." The U.S. Declaration of Independence, which was authored by Jefferson, states that governments exist to protect our unalienable right to *the pursuit of happiness.* Then, wouldn't governments also exist to facilitate the health that is required for the pursuit and attainment of happiness? It is true that a government governs best when it governs least. Yet, included in the "least" is the mandate to ensure the health of the nation. Take solace in Winston Churchill's assessment: "The American people will inevitably do the right thing, but only after they have tried all other alternatives." Why can't we do the right thing now? Many are already helping. Why can't we all help move the transformation forward by what ever means or light that God has given us?

This transformation involves neither conflict nor opposition, but

Self-realization. Soon we will recognize that the keys to health rest not in the hands of medical professionals, but in our own hearts and minds. We will cease to be slaves of high technology, powerful drugs, and multinational corporations. We will be liberated by our discovery of how to harness nature's deepest balance, harmony, and order within ourselves. This revolution involves nothing new; it is a return to truths that have always existed. We were always causing our own health or illness. Some of the most ancient traditions of medical knowledge appear to have preserved a comprehensive understanding of how to restore balance and maintain human health. We will learn from them with open minds and hearts. Instead of the narrow fragmented medical systems of today, we will discover a complete science of restoring balance to the individual's consciousness, mind, body, behavior, environment, and their interconnections. We will integrate the best of modern medicine with the best of traditional, complementary, and alternative medicine. This is how to reduce our high medical expenses.

Health is extremely important. It is the basis of any successful civilization or individual life. The wisest men of old have said that all human experience is *self-referral*. That is why Socrates and other great teachers have urged, "Know Thy Self." This is a self-evident truth. When all things are considered, reconnecting with our higher Self and re-establishing self-referral awareness is the best way to help maintain physical and mental health and fulfill our needs on all levels.

To help preserve and enhance the God-given gift of physical, mental, and spiritual health of our nations and world is one of the highest and most noble goals to which any of us might aspire. Fulfillment is often achieved by living for something larger than ourselves. Shall we work for our mutual benefit by improving medical systems on a really profound scale? If we do this, future generations will have a glorious destiny beyond our most optimistic imagining. Let us make the best future for our planet a reality, not just a hope.

With expanded disease prevention and improved health, our national medical budgets should be less than 3% of gross national product, instead of the current levels. This will free huge sums of money to help solve problems in other important areas of life. Prosperity, peace, and happiness could then more easily flourish for all. Best wishes to everyone for perfect health and low medical expenses. May God be with you!

# Appendix I

# Recommended Books on the U.S. Medical System and Pharmaceutical Industry

*HOW DOCTORS THINK* by Jerome Groopman, M.D., New York: Houghton Mifflin, 2007.

*WHO KILLED HEALTH CARE? America's $2 Trillion Medical Problem — And the Consumer-Driven Cure* by Regina Herzlinger, Ph.D., New York: McGraw-Hill, 2007.

*OVERDO$ED AMERICA: The Broken Promise of American Medicine* by John Abramson, M.D., New York: HarperCollins Publishers, 2004.

*THE TRUTH ABOUT DRUG COMPANIES: How They Deceive Us and What to Do About It* by Marcia Angell, M.D., New York: Random House, 2004.

*POWERFUL MEDICINES: The Benefits, Risks, and Costs of Prescription Drugs* by Jerry Avorn, M.D., New York: Alfred A. Knopf, 2004.

*ON THE TAKE: How America's Complicity with Big Business Can Endanger Your Health* by Jerome P. Kassirer, M.D., New York: Oxford University Press, 2004.

*CANCER-GATE: How to Win the Losing Cancer War* by Samuel S. Epstein, M.D., Amityville, NY: Baywood Publishing Co., 2005

*HOPE OR HYPE: The Obsession with Medical Advances and the High Cost of False Promises* by Richard A. Deyo, M.D. and Donald L Patrick, Ph.D., New York: AMACOM, 2005.

*BIG FAT LIARS: How Politicians, Corporations, and the Media Use Science and Statistics to Manipulate the Public* by Morris E. Chafetz,

M.D., Nashville, Tenn: Nelson Current, 2005.

*CRITICAL CONDITION: How Health Care in America Became Big Business & Bad Medicine* by Donald L. Barlett and James B. Steele, New York: Doubleday (Random House), 2004.

*INTERNAL BLEEDING: The Truth Behind America's Terrifying Epidemic of Medical Mistakes* by Robert M. Wachter, M.D. and Kaveh G. Shojania, M.D., New York: Rugged Land, LLC, 2004.

*SELLING SICKNESS: How the World's Biggest Pharmaceutical Companies Are Turning Us All Into Patients* by Ray Moynihan and Alan Cassels, New York: Nation Books, 2005.

*GENERATION RX: How Prescription Drugs Are Altering American Lives, Minds, and Bodies* by Greg Critser, New York: Houghton Mifflin, 2005.

*EVIDENCE OF HARM: Mercury in Vaccines and the Autism Epidemic: A Medical Controversy* by David Kirby, New York: St. Martin's Press, 2005.

*THE $800 MILLION PILL: The Truth Behind the Cost of New Drugs* by Merrill Goozner, Berkeley, CA: University of California Press, 2004.

*OVER DOSE: The Case Against the Drug Companies* by Jay S. Cohen, M.D., New York: Jeremy P. Tarcher/Penguin, 2004.

*THE BIG FIX: How the Pharmaceutical Industry Rips Off American Consumers* by Katherine Greider, New York: Public Affairs, 2003.

*ONE NATION, UNINSURED: Why the U.S. Has No National Health Insurance* by Jill Quadagno, Ph.D., New York: Oxford University Press, 2005.

*MONEY-DRIVEN MEDICINE: The Real Reason Health Care Costs So Much.* by Maggie Mahar, New York: HarperCollins, 2006.

*THE LAST WELL PERSON: How to Stay Well Despite the Health-Care System.* by Nortin M. Hadler, M.D., Montreal & Kingston: McGill-Queen's University Press, 2005.

*THE END OF MODERN MEDICINE: Biomedical Science Under a Microscope* by Laurence Foss, Albany, NY, State University of New York Press, 2002.

*DEATH BY MEDICINE* by Gary Null, Ph.D., C. Dean, M. Feldman, D. Rasio, D. Smith. Available at: http://www.garynull.com/documents/iatrogenic/deathbymedicine/Dea thByMedicine.pdf.

# Appendix II

# Recommended Reading on Complementary and Alternative Medicine

Schneider, R.H., Fields, J.Z. *Total Heart Health*. Laguna Beach, CA: Basic Health Publications, 2006.

Lonsdorf, N. *The Ageless Woman: Natural Health and Beauty after Forty with Maharishi Ayurveda*. Ann Arbor, MI: MCD Century Publications, 2004.

Rotblatt, M., Ziment, I. *Evidence-based Herbal Medicine*. Philadelphia: Hanley & Belfus, 2002.

Ernst, E. *The Desktop Guide to Complementary and Alternative Medicine: An Evidence-Based Approach*. London: Harcourt Publishing Ltd. (Mosby), 2001.

Pelletier, K.R. *The Best Alternative Medicine: What Works? What Does Not?* New York: Simon & Schuster, 2000.

Ernst, E. *Complementary Medicine: A Critical Appraisal*. Oxford: Butterworth-Heinemann, 1996.

Lewith, G., Kenyon, J., Lewis, P. *Complementary Medicine: An Integrated Approach*. Oxford: Oxford University Press, 1996 (Oxford General Practice Series).

Vickers, A.J., ed. *Examining Complementary Medicine*. Cheltenham: Stanley Thornes, 1998.

Vincent, C., Furnham, A. *Complementary Medicine: A Research Perspective*. London: Wiley, 1997.

Woodham, A., Peters, D. *An Encyclopaedia of Complementary Medicine*. London: Dorling Kindersley, 1997.

# References

## Introduction

1. Boyd J. Thomas Jefferson's letter to Thomas Mann Randolph, Jr. on July 6, 1787. *The Papers of Thomas Jefferson*. 1955;11:558.

2. Banthin JS, Bernard DM. Changes in financial burdens for health care: National estimates for the population younger than 65 years, 1996 to 2003. *Journal of the American Medical Association*. 2006;296: 2712–2719.

3. Havighurst CC, Richman BD. *Distributive Injustice(s) in American Health Care:* Duke University Law School January 2007. Research Report No. 140.

4. Institute of Medicine. *Insuring America's Health: Principles and Recommendations*. Washington, DC: National Academies Press; January 2004.

5. Thorpe KE. The rise in health care spending and what to do about it. *Health Affairs*. 2005;24(6):1436–1445.

6. Page S. Climate is right for health care reform. *USA Today*. December 30, 2002: 1A.

7. Carlton J. Schwarzenegger Wrestles With Health Care. *Wall Street Journal*. Dec. 21, 2006: A6.

8. Emanuel EJ, Fuchs VR. Beyond Health-Care Band-Aids. *Washington Post*. Feb. 7, 2007: A17.

# Chapter 1

1. Levitt SD, Dubner SJ. *FREAKONOMICS: A Rogue Economist Explores the Hidden Side of Everything, Revised and Expanded Edition.* New York: William Morrow; 2006.

2. Sager A, Socolar D. *Health Costs Absorb One-Quarter of Economic Growth, 2000 - 2005.* Boston, Massachusetts: Boston University School of Public Health; Feb. 9, 2005.

3. Himmelstein DU, Woolhandler S, Wolfe SM. Administrative waste in the U.S. health care system in 2003: The cost to the nation, the states, and the District of Columbia, with state-specific estimates of potential savings. *International Journal of Health Services.* 2004; 34(1):79–86.

4. Woolhandler S, Campbell T, Himmelstein DU. Costs of health care administration in the United States and Canada. *New England Journal of Medicine.* 2003;349(8):768–775.

5. Woolhandler S, Himmelstein DU. The high-costs of for-profit care. *Journal of the Canadian Medical Association.* 2004;170(12):1814–1815.

6. Woolhandler S, Campbell T, Himmelstein DU. Health care administration in the United States and Canada: Micromanagement, macro costs. *International Journal of Health Services.* 2004;34(1):65–78.

7. *The World Health Report 2000, Health Systems: Improving Performance.* Geneva, Switzerland: World Health Organization; 2000.

8. Whalen JP. Health care in America: Lost opportunities amid plenty. *Qualitative Health Research.* 2003;13(6):857–870.

9. Evans DB, Tandon A, Murray CJL, Lauer JA. Comparative efficiency of national health systems: Cross national econometric analysis. *British Medical Journal.* 2001;323:307–310.

10. *World Health Statistics 2006.* Geneva, Switzerland: World Health Organization; 2006.

11. Marmot M. *Status Syndrome: How your social standing directly affects your health and life expectancy.* London: Bloomsbury; 2004.

12. Marmot M, Wilkinson RH. *Social Determinants of Health.* 2nd ed. New York/London: Oxford University Press; 2006.

13. Evans RG, Stoddart GL. Consuming research, producing policy? *American Journal of Public Health.* 2003;93(3):371–379.

14. McKinlay JB, McKinlay SM. The questionable contribution of medical measures to the decline of mortality in the United States in the twentieth century. *Milbank Memorial Fund Quarterly.* 1977; Summer:405–428.

15. McKinlay JB, McKinlay SM, Beaglehole R. A review of the evidence concerning the impact of medical measures on recent mortality and morbidity in the United States. *International Journal of Health Services.* 1989;19(2):181–208.

16. McKeown T. Determinants of Health. *Human Nature.* 1978;April: 60–67.

17. McKeown T. *The Role of Medicine: Dream, Mirage or Nemesis?* Princeton, New Jersey: Princeton University Press; 1979.

18. McKeown T. *The Origins of Human Disease.* Oxford, UK: Basil Blackwell; 1988.

19. McKeown T, Record RG, Turner RD. An interpretation of the decline in mortality in England and Wales during the twentieth century. *Population Studies.* 1975;29(3):391–422.

20. Garrett L. *Betrayal of Trust: The Collapse of Global Public Health.* New York: Hyperion; 2000.

21. Sagan LA. *The Health of Nations: The True Causes of Sickness and Well-being.* New York: Basic Books; 1987.

22. *For a Healthy Nation: Returns on Investment in Public Health.* Washington, D.C.: Public Health Service, U.S. Dept. of Health and Human Services; 1994.

23. Mansfield E. *Economics: Principles/Problems/Decisions.* 7th ed. New York: W.W. Norton and Company; 1992.

24. Holtz TH, Holmes S, Stonington S, Eisenberg L. Health is still social: Contemporary examples in the age of the genome. *PLoS Medicine.* 2006;3(10):1663–1666.

25. Wildavsky A. Doing better and feeling worse: The political pathology of health policy. *Daedalus.* 1977;106(1):105–123.

26. Wennberg JE, Fisher ES, Skinner JS. Geography and the debate over Medicare reform. *Health Affairs.* 2002;Web-Exclusive(Feb. 13):W96–W114.

27. Fisher ES, Wennberg DE, Stukel TA, Gottlieb DJ, Lucas FL, Pinder EL. The implications of regional variations in Medicare spending. Part 1: The content, quality, and accessibility of care. *Annals of Internal Medicine.* 2003;138(4):273–287.

28. Fisher ES, Wennberg DE, Stukel TA, Gottlieb DJ, Lucas FL, Pinder EL. The implications of regional variations in Medicare spending. Part 2: Health outcomes and satisfaction with care. *Annals of Internal Medicine.* 2003;138(4):288–298.

## Chapter 2

1. Engel GL. The need for a new medical model: A challenge for biomedicine. *Science.* 1977;196(4286):129–136.

2. Churchman CW. *The Systems Approach, Revised and Updated.* New York: Laurel (Dell Publishing); 1979.

3. Dacher ES. A systems theory approach to an expanded medical model: A challenge for biomedicine. *Journal of Alternative and Complementary Medicine.* 1995;1(2):187–196.

4. Wade DT, Halligan PW. Do biomedical models of illness make for good healthcare systems? *British Medical Journal.* 2004;329(Dec. 11):1398–1401.

5. Abramson J. *OVERDO$ED AMERICA: The Broken Promise of American Medicine.* New York: HarperCollins Publishers; 2004.

6. Dubos R. *The Mirage of Health: Utopias, Progress and Biological Change.* New York: Harper & Row; 1959.

7. Whitbeck C. A Theory of Health. In: Caplan AL, Engelhardt J, Tristram H, McCartney JJ, eds. *Concepts of Health and Disease: Interdisciplinary Perspectives.* Reading, MA: Addison-Wesley; 1981.

8. Krieger N. Epidemiology and the web of causation: Has anyone seen the spider? *Social Science and Medicine.* 1993;39(7):887–903.

9. Foss L. *The End of Modern Medicine: Biomedical Science Under a Microscope.* Albany, NY: State University of New York Press; 2002.

10. Greaves D. Reflections on a new medical cosmology. *Journal of Medical Ethics.* 2002;28:81–85.

11. Dossey L. *Space, Time & Medicine.* Boston: New Science Library; 1985.

12. Foss L, Rothenberg K. *The Second Medical Revolution.* Boston: New Science Library; 1987.

13. McWhinney IR. Forward. In: Foss L, *The End of Medicine: Biomedical Science Under a Microscope.* Albany, NY: State University of New York; 2002.

14. *To Err Is Human: Building a Safer Health System.* Institute of Medicine of the National Academies. Washington, DC: National Academy Press; 1999.

15. Wachter RM, Shojania KG. *Internal Bleeding: The Truth Behind America's Terrifying Epidemic of Medical Mistakes.* New York: Rugged Land; 2004.

16. *Five Years After IOM Report on Medical Errors, Nearly Half of All Consumers Worry About Safety of Their Health Care.* Kaiser Family Foundation. Available at: http://www.kff.org/kaiserpolls/ pomr-111704nr.cfm?RenderForPrint=1. Accessed Nov. 18, 2004.

17. Null G, Dean C, Feldman M, Rasio D, Smith D. *Death by Medicine.* Available at: http://www.garynull.com/documents/iatrogenic/deathbymedicine/DeathByMedicine.pdf. Accessed March 22, 2004.

18. Starfield B. Is US health really the best in the world? *Journal of the American Medical Association.* 2000;284(4):483–485.

19. Starfield B. Deficiencies in US medical care. *Journal of the American Medical Association.* 2000;284(17):2184–2185.

20. Hoffman C, Rice D, Sung H-Y. Persons with chronic conditions: Their prevalence and costs. *Journal of the American Medical Association.* 1996;276:1473–1479.

21. Culliton BJ. Extracting knowledge from science: A conversation with Elias Zerhouni. *Health Affairs.* 2006;25(March 9 online at www.healthaffairs.org):w94–w103.

22. Carmen IH. A death in the laboratory: The politics of the Gelsinger aftermath. *Molecular Therapy.* 2001;3:425–428.

23. Buttner P, Mosig S, Lechtermann A, Funke H, Mooren FC. Exercise affects gene expression profiles of human white blood cells. *Journal of Applied Physiology.* 2007;102(1):26–36.

24. Booth FW, Neufer PD. Exercise controls gene expression. *American Scientist.* 2005;93(Jan. - Feb.):29–35.

25. Ling C, Poulsen P, Carlsson E, et al. Multiple environmental and genetic factors influence skeletal muscle PGC-1a and PGC-1b gene expression in twins. *Journal of Clinical Investigation.* 2004;114(10): 1518–1526.

26. Booth FW, Chakravarthy MV, Spangenburg EE. Exercise and gene expression: Physiological regulation of the human genome through physical exercise. *Journal of Physiology.* 2002;543(2):399–411.

27. Rampon C, Jiang CH, Dong H, et al. Effects of environmental enrichment on gene expression in the brain. *Proceedings of the National Academy of Sciences.* 2000;97(23):12880–12884.

28. Bray MS. Genomics, genes, and environmental interaction: The role of exercise. *Journal of Applied Physiology.* 2000;88:788–792.

29. Guzowski JF, McNaughton BL, Barnes CA, Worley PF. Environmental-specific expression of the immediate-early gene Arc in hippocampal neuronal ensembles. *Nature Neuroscience.* 1999; 2(12):1120–1124.

30. Sudano JJ, Baker DW. Explaining US racial/ethnic disparities in health decline and mortality in late middle age: The roles of socioeconomic status, health behaviors, and health insurance. *Social Science and Medicine.* 2006;62:909–922.

31. Marmot M, Wilkinson RH. *Social Determinants of Health.* 2nd ed. New York/London: Oxford University Press; 2006.

32. Marmot M. *Status Syndrome: How your social standing directly affects your health and life expectancy.* London: Bloomsbury; 2004.

33. Pollitt RA, Rose KM, Kaufman JS. Evaluating the evidence for models of life course socioeconomic factors and cardiovascualr outcomes: A systematic review. *BMC Public Health.* January 20 2005;5(7):1-13.

34. Hemingway H, Marmot M. Psychosocial factors in the etiology and prognosis of coronary heart disease: Systematic review of prospective cohort studies. *British Medical Journal.* 1999;319:1460–1467.

35. McDonough P, Duncan GJ, Williams D, House J. Income dynamics and adult mortality in the United States, 1972 through 1989. *American Journal of Public Health.* 1997;87:1476–1483.

36. Wilkinson RG. *Unhealthy Societies: The Afflictions of Inequality.* London, England: Routledge; 1996.

37. Sapolsky R. *Stress, the Aging Brain, and the Mechanisms of Neuron Death.* Cambridge, MA: MIT Press; 1992.

38. Weiner H. *Perturbing the Organism: The Biology of Stressful Experience.* Chicago: University of Chicago Press; 1992.

39. Segerstrom SC, Miller GE. Psychological stress and the human immune system: A meta-analytic study of 30 years of inquiry. *Psychological Bulletin.* 2004;130(4):601–630.

40. Chrousos G, Gold P. The concepts of stress and stress system disorders: Overview of physical and behavioral homeostasis. *Journal of the American Medical Association.* 1992;267(9):1244–1252.

41. Chrousos G. The hypothalamic-pituitary-adrenal axis and immune-meditated inflammation. *Journal of the American Medical Association.* 1995;332(20):1351–1362.

42. Mahar M. *Money-Driven Medicine: The Real Reason Health Care Costs So Much.* New York: HarperCollins; 2006.

## Chapter 3

1. Goldsmith J. Death of a Paradigm: The Challenge of Competition. *Health Affairs.* 1984;3(3):5–19.

2. Eisenberg DM, Davis RB, Ettner SL, et al. Trends in alternative medicine use in the United States, 1990–1997. *Journal of the American Medical Association.* 1998;280(18):1569–1575.

3. Barnes PM, Powell-Griner E, McFann K, Nahin RL. Complementary and alternative medicine use among adults: United States, 2002. *Advanced Data.* 2004;343(May 27):1–19.

4. Wilk CA. *Medicine, Monopolies, and Malice.* Garden City Park, NY: Avery Publishing Group; 1996.

5. Wolinsky H, Brune T. *The Serpent on the Staff: The Unhealthy Politics of the American Medical Association.* New York: G.P. Putnam's Sons; 1994.

6. Guylaine L. *The Medical Mafia.* Waterloo, Quebec, Canada: Here's The Key, Inc.; 1995.

7. Carter JP. *Racketeering in Medicine: The Suppression of Alternatives.* Charlottesville, Virginia: Hampton Roads Publishing Co.; 1992.

8. Dubos R. *The Mirage of Health: Utopias, Progress and Biological Change.* New York: Harper & Row; 1959.

9. Hagelin JS. *Manual for a Perfect Government.* Fairfield, Iowa: Maharishi University of Management Press; 1998.

10. Leaf A. Preventive medicine for our ailing health care system. *Journal of the American Medical Association.* 1993;269(5):616–618.

11. Greaves D. Reflections on a new medical cosmology. *Journal of Medical Ethics.* 2002;28:81–85.

# Chapter 4

1. Pelletier KR, Astin JA, Haskell WL. Current trends in the integration and reimbursement of complementary and alternative medicine by managed care organizations (MCOs) and insurance providers: 1998 update and cohort analysis. *American Journal of Health Promotion.* 1999;14(2):125–133.

2. Furnham A. The psychology of complementary and alternative medicine. *Evidence-Based Integrative Medicine.* 2003;1(1):57–64.

3. Bodeker G, Kronenberg F. A public health agenda for traditional, complementary, and alternative medicine. *American Journal of Public Health.* 2002;92(10):1582–1591.

4. Barnes PM, Powell–Griner E, McFann K, Nahin RL. Complementary and alternative medicine use among adults: United States, 2002. *Advanced Data.* 2004;343(May 27):1–19.

5. Eisenberg DM, Davis RB, Ettner SL, et al. Trends in alternative medicine use in the United States, 1990–1997. *Journal of the American Medical Association.* 1998;280(18):1569–1575.

6. Eisenberg DM, Kessler RC, Foster C, Norlock FE, Calkins DR, Delbanco TL. Unconventional medicine in the United States: Prevalence, costs, and patterns of use. *New England Journal of Medicine.* 1993;328(4):246–252.

7. Schappert SM. *National Ambulatory Medical Care Survey: 1990 Summary.* Hyattsville, MD: National Center for Health Statistics; 1992. 213:1–11.

8. Woodwell DA. *National Ambulatory Medical Care Survey: 1996 Summary.* Hyattsville, MD: National Center for Health Statistics; 1997. 295:1–25.

9. Astin JA, Marie A, Pelletier KR, Hansen E, Haskell WL. A review of the incorporation of complementary and alternative medicine by mainstream physicians. *Archives of Internal Medicine.* 1998;158 (21):2303–2310.

10. Eisenberg DM, Kessler RC, Van Rompay MI, et al. Perceptions about complementary therapies relative to conventional therapies among adults who use both: Results from a national survey. *Annals of Internal Medicine.* 2001;135(5):344–351.

11. Astin JA. Why patients use alternative medicine: Results of a national study. *Journal of the American Medical Association.* 1998;279(19):1548–1553.

12. Astin JA, Pelletier KR, Marie A, Haskell WL. Complementary and alternative medicine use among elderly persons: One-year analysis of a Blue Shield Medicare supplement. *Journal of Gerontology A, Biological and Medical Sciences.* 2000;55(1):M4–9.

13. Druss BG, Rosenheck RA. Association between use of unconventional therapies and conventional medical services. *Journal of the American Medical Association.* 1999;282(7):651–656.

14. Paramore LC. Use of alternative therapies: Estimates from the 1994 Robert Wood Johnson Foundation national access to care survey. *Journal of Pain Symptoms & Management.* 1997;13(2):83–89.

15. Blais R, Maïga A, Aboubacar A. How different are users and non-users of alternative medicine? *Canadian Journal of Public Health.* 1997;88(3):159–162.

16. Millar WJ. Use of alternative health care practitioners by Canadians. *Canadian Journal of Public Health.* 1997; 88(3):154–158.

17. Kelner M, B. Wellman. Health care and consumer choice: Medical and alternative therapies. *Social Science and Medicine.* 1997;45(2):203–212.

18. Wetzel MS, Kaptchuk TJ, Haramati A, Eisenberg DM. Complementary and alternative medical therapies: Implications for medical education. *Annals of Internal Medicine.* 2003;138(3):191–196.

19. Abramson J. *OVERDO$ED AMERICA: The Broken Promise of American Medicine.* New York: HarperCollins Publishers; 2004.

20. Deyo RA, Patrick DL. *Hope or Hype: The Obsession with Medical Advances and the High Cost of False Promises.* New York: AMACOM; 2005.

21. Moynihan R, Cassels A. *Selling Sickness: How the World's Biggest Pharmaceutical Companies Are Turning Us All Into Patients.* New York: Nation Books (Avalon Publishing Group); 2005.

22. Epstein SS. *Cancer-Gate: How to Win the Losing Cancer War.* Amityville, NY: Baywood Publishing Company, Inc.; 2005.

23. Angell M. *The Truth About Drug Companies: How They Deceive Us and What to Do About It.* New York: Random House; 2004.

24. Avorn J. *Powerful Medicines: The Benefits, Risks, and Costs of Prescription Drugs.* New York: Alfred A. Knopf; 2004.

25. Kassirer JP. *On the Take: How America's Complicity with Big Business Can Endanger Your Health.* New York: Oxford University Press; 2004.

26. Cohen JS. *Over Dose: The Case Against the Drug Companies.* New York: Jeremy P. Tarcher/Penguin; 2004.

27. Barlett DL, Steele JB. *Critical Condition: How Health Care in America Became Big Business and Bad Medicine.* New York: Doubleday (Random House); 2004.

28. Greider K. *The Big Fix: How the Pharmaceutical Industry Rips Off American Consumers.* New York: Public Affairs; 2003.

29. Pelletier K. Conventional and integrative medicine—evidence based? *Focus on Alternative and Complementary Therapies.* 2003; 8(1): 3–6.

30. Smith R. Where is the wisdom?...The poverty of medical evidence. *British Medical Journal.* 1991;303:798–799.

31. Dalen J. Conventional and unconventional medicine: Can they be integrated? *Archives of Internal Medicine.* 1998;158:1–4.

32. Koretz RL. Is alternative medicine alternative science? *Journal of Laboratory and Clinical Medicine.* 2002;139(6):329–333.

33. Hadler NM. *The Last Well Person: How to Stay Well Despite the Health-Care System.* Montreal & Kingston: McGill-Queen's University Press; 2005.

34. Schneider RH, Fields JZ. *Total Heart Health: How to Prevent and Reverse Heart Disease with the Maharishi Vedic Approach to Health.* Laguna Beach, CA: Basic Health Publications; 2006.

35. Wente MN, Seiler CM, Uhl W, Buchler MW. Perspectives of evidence-based surgery. *Digestive Surgery.* 2003;20(4):263–269.

36. Timmermans A, Mauck A. The promises and pitfalls of evidence-based medicine. *Health Affairs.* 2005;24(1):18–28.

37. Steinberg EP, Luce BR. Evidence Based? Caveat Emptor! *Health Affairs.* 2005;24(1):80–92.

38. Konner M. *Medicine at the Crossroads.* New York: Vintage (Random House); 1994.

39. White K. *Medicine & Culture: Varieties of Treatment in the United States, England, West Germany, and France.* New York: Henry Holt and Co.; 1988.

40. McPherson K. International differences in medical care practice. *Health Care Financing Review.* 1989;Annual Supplement:9–20.

41. Shekelle PG. *The Use and Costs of Chiropractic Care in the Health Insurance Experiment.* Santa Monica, CA: RAND; 1994.

42. Legorreta AP, Metz RD, Nelson CF, Ray S, Chernicoff HO, DiNubile NA. Comparative analysis of individuals with and without chiropractic coverage. *Archives of Internal Medicine.* 2004;164(18): 1985–1992.

43. OECD Health Data 2005. Washington, DC: Organization for Economic Co-operation and Development; 2006.

44. Manga P, Angus DE, Papadopoulos C, Swan WR. *A Study to Examine the Effectiveness and Cost-Effectiveness of Chiropractic Management of Low-Back Pain.* Richmond Hill, Ontario, Canada: Kenilworth Publishing; 1993.

45. Culliton PD. *Current Utilization of Acupunture by United States Patients.* Bethesda, MD: National Institutes of Health Consensus Panel; Nov. 3 1997.

46. Pearl D, Schillinger E. Acupuncture: its use in medicine. *Western Journal of Medicine.* 1999;171:176–180.

47. Ma S–X. Neurobiology of acupuncture: Toward CAM. *eCAM.* 2004;1(1):41–47.

48. Vickers AJ, Rees RW, Zollman CE, et al. Migraine treatments now and in the future. *Headache.* 2004;44(8):846–850.

49. Lee H, Ernst E. Acupuncture for labor pain management: A systematic review. *American Journal of Obstetrics and Gynecology.* 2004; 191(5):1573–1579.

50. Meng CF, Wang D, Ngeow J, Lao L, Peterson M, Paget S. Acupuncture for chronic low back pain in older adults: A randomized, controlled trial. *Rheumatology.* 2003;42:1508–1517.

51. Fink M, Wolkenstein E, Karst M, Gehrke A. Acupuncture in chronic epicondylitis. *Rheumatology.* 2002;41:205–209.

52. Wonderling D, Vickers AJ, Grieve R, McCarney R. Cost effectiveness analysis of a randomised trial of acupuncture for chronic headache in primary care. *British Medical Journal.* Available at: BMJ, doi:10.1136/bmj.38033.896505.EB. Accessed Dec. 17, 2004.

53. Kaptchuk TJ. Acupuncture: Theory, efficacy, and practice. *Annals of Internal Medicine.* 2002;136:374–383.

54. Wolsko PM, Eisenberg DM, Davis RB, Phillips RS. Use of mind-body medical therapies: Results of a national survey. *Journal of General Internal Medicine.* 2004;19:43–50.

55. *Alternative Medicine: Expanding Medical Horizons.* National Institutes of Health. Washington, DC: Government Printing Office; 1994.

56. Pelletier KR. Mind-body medicine in ambulatory care: An evidence-based assessment. *Journal of Ambulatory Care Management.* 2004;27(1):25–42.

57. Astin JA, Shapiro SL, Eisenberg DM, Forys KL. Mind-body medicine: State of the science, implications for practice. *Journal of the American Board of Family Practitioners.* 2003;16(2):131–147.

58. Blumenthal JA, Jiang W, Babyak MA, et al. Stress management and exercise training in cardiac patients with myocardial ischemia. Effects on prognosis and evaluation of mechanisms. *Archives of Internal Medicine.* 1997;157:2213–2223.

# Chapter 5

1. Cryer B, McCraty R, Childre D. Pull the plug on stress. *Harvard Business Review.* 2003;81(7):102–107, 118.

2. Anderson DR, Whitmer RW, Goetzel RZ, Ozminkowski RJ, Wasserman J, Serxner S. The relationship between modifiable health risks and group-level health care expenditures. *American Journal of Health Promotion.* 2000;15(1):45–52.

3. Chrousos G, Gold P. The concepts of stress and stress system disorders: overview of physical and behavioral homeostasis. *Journal of the American Medical Association.* 1992;267(9):1244–1252.

4. Sapolsky RM. *Why Zebras Don't Get Ulcers.* 3rd ed. New York: Henry Holt & Company; 2004.

5. Segerstrom SC, Miller GE. Psychological stress and the human immune system: A meta-analytic study of 30 years of inquiry. *Psychological Bulletin.* 2004;130(4):601–630.

6. Sapolsky R.M. *Stress, the Aging Brain, and the Mechanisms of Neuron Death.* Cambridge, MA: MIT Press; 1992.

7. Weiner H. *Perturbing the Organism: The Biology of Stressful Experience.* Chicago: University of Chicago Press; 1992.

8. Chrousos G. The hypothalamic-pituitary-adrenal axis and immune-meditated inflammation. *Journal of the American Medical Association.* 1995;332(20):1351–1362.

9. Wolff JL, Starfield B, Anderson G. Prevalence, expenditures, and complications of multiple chronic conditions in the elderly. *Archives of Internal Medicine.* 2002;162(20):2269–2276.

10. Hoffman C, Rice D, Sung H–Y. Persons with chronic conditions: Their prevalence and costs. *Journal of the American Medical Association.* 1996;276:1473–1479.

11. Jones DL, Tanigawa T, Weiss SM. Stress management and workplace disability in the US, Europe and Japan. *Journal of Occupational Health.* 2003;45:1–7.

12. Pelletier KR, Lutz R. Healthy people—healthy business: A critical review of stress management programs in the workplace. *American Journal of Health Promotion.* 1988;2(3):5–12.

13. Tucker LA, Clegg AG. Differences in health care costs and utilization among adults with selected lifestyle-related risk factors. *American Journal of Health Promotion.* 2002;16(4):225–233.

14. Shields M. *Stress, Health, and the Benefit of Social Support.* Ottawa, Canada: Statistics Canada; January 2004.

15. Goetzel RZ, Anderson DR, Whitmer RW, et al. The relationship between modifiable health risks and health care expenditures: An analysis of the multi-employer HERO health risk and cost database. *Journal of Occupational and Environmental Medicine.* 1998;40(10):843–854.

16. Wallace RK. *The Neurophysiology of Enlightenment.* Fairfield, IA: MIU Press; 1986.

17. Wallace RK. *The Physiology of Consciousness.* Fairfield, IA: Institute of Science, Technology and Public Policy and MIU Press; 1993.

18. Jevning R, Wallace RK, Beidebach M. The physiology of meditation: A Review. A wakeful hypometabolic integrated response. *Neuroscience and Biobehavioral Reviews.* 1992;16:415–424.

19. Wallace RK. Physiological effects of Transcendental Meditation. *Science.* 1970;167:1751–1754.

20. Wallace RK, Benson H. The physiology of meditation. *Scientific American.* 1972;226(2):84–90.

21. Maharishi Mahesh Yogi. *Science of Being and Art of Living: Transcendental Meditation.* New York: Meridan; 1995.

22. Nader T. *Human Physiology: Expression of Veda and the Vedic Literature.* 4th ed. Vlodrop, The Netherlands; 2000.

23. Schneider RH, Fields JZ. *Total Heart Health: How to Prevent and Reverse Heart Disease with the Maharishi Vedic Approach to Health.* Laguna Beach, CA: Basic Health Publications; 2006.

24. Orme-Johnson DW, Walton K. All approaches to preventing and reversing effects of stress are not the same. *American Journal of Health Promotion.* 1998;12(5):297–299.

25. Eppley K, Abrams A, Shear J. Differential effects of relaxation techniques on trait anxiety. *Journal of Clinical Psychology.* 1989; 45(6): 957–974.

26. Oates RM. *Celebrating the Dawn.* New York: Putnam's Sons; 1976.

27. Walton KG, Levitsky D. A neuroendocrine mechanism for the reduction of drug abuse and addictions by Transcendental Meditation. *Alcohol Treatment Quarterly.* 1994;11(1/2):89–117.

28. Walton KG, Pugh NDC, Gelderloos P, MaCrae P. Stress reduction and preventing hypertension: Preliminary support for a psychoneuroendocrine mechanism. *Journal of Alternative & Complementary Medicine.* 1995;1(3):263–283.

29. Jevning R, Wilson A, Davidson J. Adrenocortical activity during meditation. *Hormones and Behavior.* 1978;10:54–60.

30. Jevning R, Wilson A, Smith W. The Transcendental Meditation technique, adrenocortical activity and implications for stress. *Experientia.* 1978;34:618–619.

31. Subrahmanyam S, Porkodi K. Neurohumoral correlates of Transcendental Meditation. *Journal of Biomedicine.* 1980;1:73–88.

32. MacLean CRK, Walton KG, Wenneberg SR. Altered responses of cortisol, GH, TSH and testosterone to acute stress after four months' practice of Transcendental Meditation (TM). *Annals of the New York Academy of Sciences.* 1994;746:381–384.

33. Gallois P. Modifications neurophysiologiques et respiratoires lors de la practique des techniques de relaxation. *L'encephale.* 1984;10: 139–144.

34. Dillbeck MC, Orme-Johnson DW. Physiological differences between Transcendental Meditation and rest. *American Psychologist.* 1987;42:879–881.

35. Wallace RK, Silver J, Mills P, Dillbeck MC, Wagoner D. Systolic blood pressure and long-term practice of the Transcendental Meditation and TM-Sidhi program: Effects of TM on systolic blood pressure. *Psychosomatic Medicine.* 1983;45(1):41–46.

36. Alexander CN, Langer E, Newman RI, Chandler HM, Davies JL. Transcendental Meditation, mindfulness, and longevity: An experimental Study with the elderly. *Journal of Personality and Social Psychology.* 1989;57(6):950–964.

37. Cooper M, Aygen M. Effects of Transcendental Meditation on serum cholesterol and blood pressure. *Harefuah, Journal of the Israeli Medical Association.* 1978;95:1–2.

38. Schneider RH, Staggers F, Alexander CN, et al. A randomized controlled trial of stress reduction for hypertension in older African Americans. *Hypertension.* 1995;26(5):820–827.

39. Schneider RH, Alexander CN, Staggers F, et al. A randomized controlled trial of stress reduction in African Americans treated for hypertension over one year. *American Journal of Hypertension.* 2005;18(1):88–98.

40. Barnes VA, Schneider RH, Alexander CN, Rainforth M, Staggers F. Impact of Transcendental Meditation on mortality in older African Americans with hypertension—Eight year follow-up. *Journal of Social Behavior and Personality.* 2005;17(1):201–216.

41. Schneider RH, Alexander CN, Staggers F, et al. Long-term effects of stress reduction on mortality in persons >or = 55 years of age with systematic hypertension. *American Journal of Cardiology.* 2005;95(9):1060–1064.

42. Schneider RH, Alexander CN, Salerno J, W., Rainforth M, Nidich S. Stress reduction in the prevention and treatment of cardiovascular disease in African Americans: A review of controlled research on the Transcendental Meditation program. *Journal of Social Behavior and Personality.* 2005;17(1):159–180.

43. Walton K, Schneider R, Nidich S. Review of controlled research on the Transcendental Meditation Program and cardiovascular disease: Risk factors, morbidity and mortality. *Cardiology in Review.* 2004; 12(5):262–266.

44. Barnes V, Schneider R, Alexander C, Staggers F. Stress, stress reduction, and hypertension in African Americans: An updated review. *Journal of the National Medical Association.* 1997;89(7):464–476.

45. Schneider RH, Alexander CN, Wallace RK. In search of an optimal behavioral treatment for hypertension: A review and focus on Transcendental Meditation. In: Johnson E, W. G, Julius S, eds. *Personality, Elevated Blood Pressure, and Essential Hypertension.* Washington, D.C.: Hemisphere Publishing Corp; 1992:291–312.

46. Castillo-Richmond A, Schneider RH, Alexander CN, et al. Effects of stress reduction on carotid atherosclerosis in hypertensive African Americans. *Stroke.* 2000;31:568–573.

47. Zamarra JW, Schneider RH, Besseghini I, Robinson DK, Salerno JW. Usefulness of the Transcendental Meditation program in the treatment of patients with coronary artery disease. *American Journal of Cardiology.* 1996;77:867–870.

48. Jayadevappa R, Johnson JC, Bloom BS, et al. Effectiveness of transcendental meditation on functional capacity and quality of life of African Americans with congestive heart failure: A randomized control study. *Ethnicity and Disease.* 2007;17(1):72–77.

49. Barnes VA, Treiber FA, Turner R, Davis H, Strong WB. Acute effects of Transcendental Meditation on hemodynamic functioning in middle-aged adults. *Psychosomatic Medicine.* 1999;61:525–531.

50. Alexander CN, Barnes VA, Schneider RH, et al. A randomized controlled trial of stress reduction on cardiovascular and all-cause mortality in the elderly: Results of 8 and 15 year follow-ups. *Circulation* (abstract). 1996;93(3):19.

51. Rainforth MV, Schneider RH, Nidich, SI, Gaylord-King C, et al. Stress reduction programs in patients with elevated blood pressure: A systematic review and meta-analysis. *Current Hypertension Reports.* 2007; 9:520–528.

52. Alexander CN, Robinson P, Orme-Johnson DW, Schneider RH, Walton KG. The effects of Transcendental Meditation compared to other methods of relaxation and meditation in reducing risk factors, morbidity, and mortality. *Homeostasis.* 1993;35(4-5):243–264.

53. Alexander CN, Robinson P, Rainforth M. Treating and preventing alcohol, nicotine, and drug abuse through Transcendental Meditation: A review and statistical meta-analysis. *Alcohol Treatment Quarterly.* 1994;11:11–84.

54. Alexander CN, Rainforth M, Gelderloos P. Transcendental Meditation, Self-Actualization, and Psychological Health: A conceptual overview and statistical meta-analysis. *Journal of Social Behavior and Personality.* 1991;6:189–247.

55. Travis F, Wallace RK. Autonomic patterns during respiratory suspensions: Possible markers of Transcendental Consciousness. *Psychophysiology.* 1997;34:39–46.

56. Mason LI, Alexander CN, Travis FT, et al. Electrophysiological correlates of higher states of consciousness during sleep in long-term practitioners of the Transcendental Meditation program. *Sleep.* 1997;20(2):102–110.

57. Petrenko EV, Orlova TV, Lyubimov NN. Cerebral control of afferent somatosensory projections. *Bulletin of Experimental Biology and Medicine.* 1993;116(9):229–231.

58. Banquet JP. Spectral analysis of the EEG in meditation. *Electroencephalography and Clinical Neurophysiology.* 1973;35:143–151.

59. Royer A. The role of the Transcendental Meditation technique in promoting smoking cessation: A longitudinal study. *Alcoholism Treatment Quarterly.* 1994;11(1/2):221–238.

60. Brooks JS, Scarano T. Transcendental Meditation and treatment of Post-Vietnam adjustment. *Journal of Counseling and Development.* 1985;65:212–215.

61. Taub E, Steiner S, Weingarten E, Walton K. Effectiveness of broad spectrum approaches to relapse prevention in severe alcoholism: A long-term, randomized, controlled trial of Transcendental Meditation, EMG, biofeedback and electronic neurotherapy. *Alcoholism Treatment Quarterly.* 1994;11(1/2):187–220.

62. Travis F, Orme-Johnson DW. EEG coherence and power during yogic flying. *International Journal of Neuroscience.* 1990;54:1–12.

63. Orme-Johnson DW. Medical care utilization and the Transcendental Meditation program. *Psychosomatic Medicine.* 1987; 49:493–507.

64. Orme-Johnson DW, Herron RE. An innovative approach to reducing medical care utilization and expenditures. *American Journal of Managed Care.* 1997;3(1):135–144.

65. Herron RE, Cavanaugh K. Can the Transcendental Meditation program reduce the medical expenditures of older people? A longitudinal cost-reduction study in Canada. *Journal of Social Behavior and Personality.* 2005;17:415–442.

66. Fuchs VR. Health care for the elderly: How much? Who will pay for it? *Health Affairs.* 1999;18(1):11–21.

67. Dalziel WB. Demographics, aging and health care: Is there a crisis? *Canadian Medical Association Journal.* 1996;155(11):1584–1586.

68. Demers M. Factors explaining the increase in cost for physician care in Quebec's elderly population. *Canadian Medical Association Journal.* 1996;155(11):1555–1560.

69. Waldo DR, Sonnefeld ST, McKusick DR, Arnett RH. Health expenditures by age group, 1977 and 1987. *Health Care Financing Review.* 1989;10(4):111–120.

70. *The Budget and Economic Outlook.* Washington, DC: U.S. Congressional Budget Office; 2006.

71. *The Long-Term Budget Outlook.* Washington, DC: Congressional Budget Office; 2006.

72. Herron RE. The impact of Transcendental Meditation practice on medical expenditures. *Dissertation Abstracts International.* 1993;53(12): 4219–A.

73. Herron RE, Hillis SL, Mandarino JV, Orme-Johnson DW, Walton KG. The impact of the Transcendental Meditation program on government payments to physicians in Quebec. *American Journal of Health Promotion.* 1996;10(3):208–216.

74. Herron RE, Schneider RH, Mandarino JV, Alexander CN, Walton KG. Cost-effective hypertension management: Comparison of drug therapies with an alternative program. *American Journal of Managed Care.* 1996;II(4):427–437.

75. Herron RE, Hillis SL. The impact of the Transcendental Meditation program on government payments to physicians in Quebec: An update. *American Journal of Health Promotion.* 2000;14(5):284–291.

76. Schrödinger E. *What is Life? With Mind and Matter and Autobiographical Sketches.* Cambridge, UK: Cambridge University Press; 1967.

77. Eddington A. *The Nature of the Physical World.* London: Cambridge University Press; 1935.

78. Foster D. *The Philosophical Scientists.* New York: Dorset Press; 1991.

79. Klein DB. *The Concept of Consciousness: A Survey.* Lincoln, Nebraska: University of Nebraska Press; 1984.

80. Hagelin JS. *Manual for a Perfect Government.* Fairfield, Iowa: Maharishi University of Management Press; 1998.

81. Nader T, Rothenberg S, Averbach R, Charles B, Fields JZ, Schneider RH. Improvements in chronic diseases with a comprehensive natural medicine approach: A review and case series. *Behavioral Medicine.* 2000;26:34–46.

## Chapter 6

1. Evans RG. Health care as a threat to health: Defense, opulence, and the social environment. *Daedalus.* 1994;123(4):21–42.

2. Thorpe KE. The rise in health care spending and what to do about it. *Health Affairs.* 2005;24(6):1436–1445.

3. Califano JA. *America's Health Care Revolution: Who Lives? Who Dies? Who Pays?* New York, NY: Random House; 1986.

4. Spiegel JM, Yassi A. Lessons from the margins of globalization: Appreciating the Cuban health paradox. *Journal of Public Health Policy.* 2004;25(1):85–110.

5. Bennett J. *Investment in Population Health in Five OECD Countries.* Paris, France: Organisation for Economic Co-operation and Development; April 22, 2003.

6. Garrett L. *Betrayal of Trust: The Collapse of Global Public Health.* New York: Hyperion; 2000.

7. *Healthy People 2000: National Health Promotion and Disease Prevention Objectives.* Washington, DC: U.S. Department of Health and Human Services; 1991.

8. *For a Healthy Nation: Returns on Investment in Public Health.* Washington, D.C.: Public Health Service, U.S. Dept. of Health and Human Services; 1994.

9. *Healthy People 2000: Midcourse Review and 1995 Revisions.* Washington, DC: U.S. Department of Health and Human Services; 1995.

10. *Healthy people 2010: Understanding and Improving Health.* 2nd ed. Washington, DC: U.S. Government Printing Office; 2000.

11. *Healthy People: The Surgeon General's Report on Health Promotion and Disease Prevention.* Publication No. 79-55071.Washington, DC: U.S. Public Health Service; 1979.

12. *Towards High-Performing Health Systems.* Paris, France: Organisation for Economic Co-operation and Development; 2004.

13. Messonnier ML, Corso PS, Teutsch SM, Haddix AC, Harris JR. An ounce of prevention...What are the returns? *American Journal of Preventive Medicine.* 1999;16(3):248–263.

14. Pelletier KR, Lutz R. Healthy people—healthy business: A critical review of stress management programs in the workplace. *American Journal of Health Promotion.* 1988;2(3):5–12.

15. Pelletier KR. A review and analysis of the health and cost-effective outcome studies of comprehensive health promotion and disease prevention programs. *American Journal of Health Promotion.* 1991;5(4): 311–315.

16. Pelletier KR. A review and analysis of the health and cost-effective outcome studies of comprehensive health promotion and disease prevention programs at the worksite: 1991–1993 Update. *American Journal of Health Promotion.* 1993;8(1):50–62.

ROBERT E. HERRON

17. Pelletier K. A review and analysis of the health and cost-effective outcome studies of comprehensive health promotion and disease prevention programs at the worksite: 1993–1995 update. *American Journal of Health Promotion.* 1996;10(5):380–388.

18. Pelletier K. A review and analysis of the clinical and cost-effective outcome studies of comprehensive health promotion and disease management programs at the worksite: 1995–1998 update (IV). *American Journal of Health Promotion.* 1999;13(5):333–345.

19. *An Ounce of Prevention....What Are the Returns?* 2nd ed. Atlanta, Georgia: Center for Disease Control and Prevention, U.S. Department of Health and Human Services; 1999.

20. Herman WH, Hoerger TJ, Brandle M, et al. The cost-effectiveness of lifestyle modification or metformin in preventing Type 2 diabetes in adults with impaired glucose tolerance. *Annals of Internal Medicine.* 2005;142(5):323–332.

21. Harkin T. Health Care, Not Sick Care. *American Journal of Health Promotion.* 2004;19(1):1–2.

22. Estimated national spending on prevention-United States, 1988. *Morbidity and Mortality Weekly Report.* 1992;41(29):529–531.

23. Resources and priorities for chronic disease prevention and control, 1994. *Morbidity and Mortality Weekly Report.* 1997;46(13):286–295.

24. Warner KE. Cost effectiveness of smoking-cessation therapies. Interpretation of the evidence and implications for coverage. *Pharmacoeconomics.* 1997;11(6):538–549.

25. Burns DM. Reducing tobacco use: What works in the population? *Journal of Dental Education.* 2002;66(9):1051–1060.

26. Lightwood JM, Glantz SA. Short-term economic and health benefits of smoking cessation: Myocardial infarction and stroke. *Circulation.* 1997;96(4):1089–1096.

27. Mokdad AH, Marks JS, Stroup DF, Gerberding JL. Actual causes of death in the United States, 2000. *Journal of the American Medical Association.* 2004;291(10):1238–1245.

28. McGinnis J, Foege W. Actual causes of death in the United States. *Journal of the American Medical Association.* 1993;270(18):2207–2212.

29. Landrigan PJ, Schechter CB, Lipton JM, Fahs MC, Schwartz J. Environmental pollutants and disease in American children: Estimates of morbidity, mortality, and costs for lead poisoning, asthama, cancer, and developmental disabilities. *Environmental Health Perspectives.* 2002;110(7):721–728.

30. Vogt TM, Hollis JF, Lichtenstein E, Stevens VJ, Glasgow R, Whitlock E. The medical care system and prevention: The need for a new paradigm. *HMO Practice.* 1998;12(1):5–13.

**Chapter 7**

1. *The Impending Collapse of Primary Care Medicine and its Implications for the State of the Nation's Health Care.* Washington, DC: American College of Physicians; Jan. 30, 2006.

2. Bodenheimer T, Berenson RA, Rudolf P. The primary care-specialty income gap: Why it matters. *Annals of Internal Medicine.* 2007;146(4): 301–306.

3. Mullan F. The "Mona Lisa" of health policy: Primary care at home and abroad. *Health Affairs.* 1998;17(2):118–126.

4. *Primary Care: America's Health in a New Era.* Washington, DC: National Academy Press; 1996.

5. Phillips RL, Starfield B. Why does a U.S. primary care physician workforce crisis matter? *American Family Physician.* 2004;70(3): 1494–1498.

6. Starfield B, Lemke KW, Herbert R, Pavlovich WD, Anderson G. Comorbidity and the use of primary care and specialist care in the elderly. *Annals of Family Medicine.* 2005;3:215–222.

7. Bodenheimer T, Wagner EH, Grumbach K. Improving primary care for patients with chronic illness. *Journal of the American Medical Association.* 2002;288(14):1775–1779.

8. Starfield B, Shi L, Macinko J. Contribution of primary care to health systems and health. *Milbank Quarterly.* 2005;83(3):457–502.

9. Macinko J, Starfield B, Shi L. The contribution of primary care systems to health outcomes within Organization for Economic and Development (OECD) countries, 1970-1998. *Health Services Research.* 2003;38(3):831–865.

10. Starfield B, Shi L. Policy relevant determinants of health: An international perspective. *Health Policy.* 2002;60(3):201–218.

11. Starfield B. Health systems' effects on health status—financing versus the organization of services. *American Journal of Public Health.* 1995;85(10):1350–1351.

12. Shi L, Macinko J, Starfield B, et al. Primary care, infant mortality, and low birth weight in the states of the USA. *Journal of Epidemiology and Community Health.* 2004;58:374–380.

13. Shi L, Macinko J, Starfield B, Xu J, Politzer R. Primary care, income inequality, and stroke mortality in the United States. A longitudinal analysis. *Stroke.* 2003;34:1958–1964.

14. Bindman AB, Grumbach K, Osmond D, et al. Preventable hospitalizations and access to health care. *Journal of the American Medical Association.* 1995;274(4):305–311.

15. Wasson JH, Sauvigne AE, Mogielnicki RP, et al. Continuity of outpatient medical care in elderly men. A randomized trial. *Journal of the American Medical Association.* 1984;252(17):2413–2417.

16. Bindman AB, Grumbach K, Osmond D, Vranizan K, Stewart AL. Primary care and receipt of preventive services. *Journal of General Internal Medicine.* 1996;11(5):269–276.

17. Dietrich AJ, Goldberg H. Preventive content of adult primary care: Do generalists and subspecialists differ? *American Journal of Public Health.* 1984;74:223–227.

18. Ferrante JM, Gonzales EC, Pal N, Roetzheim RG. Effects of physician supply on early detection of breast cancer. *Journal of the American Board of Family Practice.* 2000;13:408–414.

19. Campbell RJ, Ramirez AM, Perez K, Roetzheim RG. Cervical cancer rates and the supply of primary care physicians in Florida. *Family Medicine.* 2003;35:60–64.

20. Roetzheim RG, Gonzalez EC, Ramirez A, Campbell R, vanDurme DJ. Primary care physician supply and colorectal cancer. *Journal of Family Practice.* 2001;50:1027–1031.

21. Greenfield S, Nelson EC, Zubkoff M, et al. Variations in resources utilization among medical specialties and systems of care. Results from the medical outcomes study. *Journal of the American Medical Association.* 1992;267(12):1624–1630.

22. Forrest C, Starfield B. The effect of first-contact care with primary care clinicians on ambulatory health care expenditures. *Journal of Family Practice.* 1996;43(1):40–48.

23. Shi L, Starfield B. The effect of primary care physician supply and income inequality on mortality among blacks and whites in U.S. metropolitan areas. *American Journal of Public Health.* 2001;91: 1246–1250.

24. Shi L, Starfield B. Primary care, income inequality, and self-rated health in the United States: A mixed-level analysis. *International Journal of Health Services.* 2000;30(3):541–555.

25. Shi L, Starfield B, Politzer R, Regan J. Primary care, self-rated health, and reductions in social disparities in health. *Health Services Research.* 2002;37:529–550.

26. Shi L, Macinko J, Starfield B, Wulu J, Regan J, Politzer R. The relationship between primary care, income inequality, and mortality in US States, 1980 – 1995. *Journal of the American Board of Family Practice.* 2003;16(5):412–422.

27. Lohr KN, Brook RH, Kamberg CJ, et al. Use of medical care in the Rand Health Insurance Experiment. Diagnosis- and service-specific analyses in a randomized controlled trial. *Medical Care.* 1986;24(supplement 9):S1–S87.

28. Starfield B. New paradigms for quality in primary care. *British Journal of General Practice.* 2001;51:303–309.

29. Starfield B, Shi L, Grover A, Macinko J. The effects of specialist supply on populations' health: Assessing the evidence. *Health Affairs.* 2005;5(March 15):w97–w107.

30. Rubenstein LV, Yano EM, Fink A, et al. Evaluation of the VA's pilot program in institutional reorganization toward primary and ambulatory care: Part I, changes in process and outcomes of care. *Academic Medicine.* 1996;71(7):772–783.

31. Reinhardt U. *Health Care in Balance.* Paper presented at: William G. Anlyan and Richard Jenrette Lecture in Health Economics and Policy; March 3, 2006; Durham, NC.

32. Delnoij D, VanMerode G, Paulus A, Groenewegen P. Does general practitioner gatekeeping curb health care expenditure? *Journal of Health Services Research & Policy.* 2000;5(1):22–26.

33. Or Z. *Health Care Reform: Controlling Spending and Increasing Efficiency.* Paris, France: Organization for Economic Cooperation and Development; 1995.

34. Gerdtham UG, Jonsson B, MacFarlan M, Oxley H. The determinants of health expenditure in the OECD countries: A pooled data analysis. *Developmental Health Economics and Public Policy.* 1998; 6:113–134.

35. Fleming MF, Mundt MP, French MT, Manwell LB, Stauffacher EA, Barry KL. Benefit-cost analysis of brief physician advice with problem drinkers in primary care settings. *Medical Care.* 2000;38(1):7–18.

36. Franks P, Fiscella K. Primary care physicians and specialists as personal physicians. Health expenditures and mortality experience. *Journal of Family Practice.* 1998;47(2):105–109.

37. DeMaeseneer JM, DePrins L, Heyerick J. Provider continuity in family medicine: Does it make a difference for total health care costs? *Annals of Family Medicine.* 2003;1:144–148.

38. Welch P, Miller ME, Welch HG, Fisher ES, Wennberg JE. Geographic variation in expenditures for physicians' services in the United States. *New England Journal of Medicine.* 1993;328(9):621–627.

39. Fuhrmans V. One Cure for High Health Costs: In-House Clinics at Companies. *Wall Street Journal.* Feb. 11, 2005: A1, A8.

40. Larson EB, Roberts KB, Grumbach K. Primary care, generalism, public good: Deja vu? Again! *Annals of Internal Medicine.* 2005;142(8): 671–674.

41. Starfield B. Is primary care essential? *Lancet.* 1994;344(Oct. 22):1129–1133.

42. *Healthy People 2000: National Health Promotion and Disease prevention Objectives.* Washington, DC: U.S. Department of Health and Human Services; 1991.

43. *Healthy People: The Surgeon General's Report on Health Promotion and Disease Prevention.* Washington, DC: U.S. Public Health Service; 1979.

44. Messonnier ML, Corso PS, Teutsch SM, Haddix AC, Harris JR. An ounce of prevention...What are the returns? *American Journal of Preventive Medicine.* 1999;16(3):248–263.

45. Berwick DM, Nolan TW. Physicians as leaders in improving health care. *Annals of Internal Medicine.* 1998;128(4):289–292.

**Chapter 8**

1. Davis K. *Transformational Change: A Ten-Point Strategy to Achieve Better Health Care for All.* New York, NY: The Commonwealth Fund; January 2005.

2. Berk ML, Monheit AC. The concentration of health expenditures: An update. *Health Affairs.* 1992;Winter:145–149.

3. Berk ML, Monheit AC. The concentration of health care expenditures, revisited. *Health Affairs.* 2001;20(2):9–18.

4. Thorpe KE, Florence CS, Joski P. Which medical conditions account for the rise in health care spending? *Health Affairs.* 2004;W4: W437–W445.

5. Fisher ES, Wennberg DE, Stukel TA, Gottlieb DJ, Lucas FL, Pinder EL. The implications of regional variations in Medicare spending. Part 1: The content, quality, and accessibility of care. *Annals of Internal Medicine.* 2003;138(4):273–287.

6. Fisher ES, Wennberg DE, Stukel TA, Gottlieb DJ, Lucas FL, Pinder EL. The implications of regional variations in Medicare spending. Part 2: Health outcomes and satisfaction with care. *Annals of Internal Medicine.* 2003;138(4):288–298.

7. Fries JF, Koop CE, Sokolov J, Beadle CE, Wright D. Beyond health promotion: reducing the need and demand for medical care. *Health Affairs.* 1998;17(2):70–84.

8. Mintzberg H. Five Ps for Strategy. In: Mintzberg H, Quinn JB, eds. *The Strategy Process: Concepts, Contexts, Cases.* 3rd ed; 1996.

9. Berk ML, Monheit AC, Hagan MM. How the U.S. spent its health care dollar, 1929-1980. *Health Affairs.* 1988;Fall:46–60.

10. Monheit AC. Persistence in health expenditures in the short run: Prevalence and consequences. *Medical Care.* 2003;41(Supplement 7):III53–III64.

11. Zook CJ, Moore FD. High-expenditure users of medical care. *New England Journal of Medicine.* 1980;302:996–1002.

12. Garfinkel SA, Riley GF, Iannacchione VG. High-expenditure users of medical care. *Health Care Financing Review.* 1988;9(4):41–52.

13. Anderson G, Knickman JR. Patterns of expenditures among high utilizers of medical care services: The experience of Medicare beneficiaries from 1974 to 1977. *Medical Care.* 1984;22(2):143–149.

14. Yen L, Edington DW, Witting P. Corporate medical claims cost distributions and factors associated with high-cost status. *Journal of Occupational Medicine.* 1994;36(5):505–515.

15. Lieberman SM, Lee J, Anderson T, Crippen DL. Reducing the growth of Medicare spending: Geographic versus patient–based strategies. *Health Affairs.* 2003;W3: W603–W613.

16. Kingery PM, Ellsworth CG, Corbett BS, Bowden RG, Brizzolara JA. High-cost analysis: A closer look at the case for work-site health promotion. *Journal of Occupational Medicine.* 1994;36(12):1341–1347.

17. McCall N, Wai HS. An analysis of the use of Medicare services by the continuously enrolled aged. *Medical Care.* 1983;21(6):567–585.

18. Alexandre LM. *Who Are the High Expenditure Cases in a Health Benefits Plan?* Brookfield, Wisconsin: International Foundation of Employee Benefit Plans; 1988.

19. Callahan CM, Stump TE, Stroupe KT, Tierney WM. Cost of health care for a community of older adults in an urban academic healthcare system. *Journal of the American Geriatrics Society.* 1998;46(11): 1371–1377.

20. Henk HJ, Katzelnick DJ, Kobak KA, et al. Medical costs attributed to depression among patients with a history of high medical expenditures in a health maintenance organization. *Archives of General Psychiatry.* 1996;53(10):899–904.

21. Goodman MJ, Roblin DW, Hornbrook MC, Mullooly JP. Persistence of health care expenses in an insured working population. *Advances in Health Economics and Health Services Research.* 1991; 12:149–173.

22. Weaver MT, Forrester BG, Brown KC, et al. Health risk influence on medical care costs and utilization among 2,898 municipal employees. *American Journal of Preventive Medicine.* 1998;15(3):250–253.

23. Zuvekas SH, Cohen JW. Prescription drugs and the changing concentration of health care expenditures. *Health Affairs.* 2007;26(1): 249–257.

24. Thorpe KE, Howard DH. The rise in spending among Medicare beneficiaries: The role of chronic disease prevalence and changes in treatment intensity. *Health Affairs.* Aug. 22 2006;25:W378–W388.

25. Fishman P, Von Korff M, Lozano P, Hecht J. Chronic care costs in managed care. *Health Affairs.* 1997;16(3):239–247.

26. Yu W, Ravelo A, Wagner TH, et al. Prevalence and costs of chronic conditions in the VA health care system. *Medical Care Research and Review.* 2003;60(Supplement 3):146S–167S.

27. Tucker LA, Clegg AG. Differences in health care costs and utilization among adults with selected lifestyle-related risk factors. *American Journal of Health Promotion.* 2002;16(4):225–233.

28. Goetzel RZ, Jacobson BH, Aldana SG, Vardell K, Yee L. Health care costs of worksite health promotion participants and non-participants. *Journal of Occupational and Environmental Medicine.* 1998; 40(4):341–346.

29. Edington DW, Yen LT, Witting P. The financial impact of changes in personal health practices. *Journal of Occupational and Environmental Medicine.* 1997;39(11):1037–1046.

30. Yen L, Edington DW, Witting P. Corporate medical claims cost distributions and factors associated with high-cost status. *Journal of Occupational Medicine.* 1994;36(5):505–515.

31. Thorpe KE, Florence CS, Howard DH, Joski P. The impact of obesity on rising medical spending. *Health Affairs.* Oct. 20 2004;4: W480–W486.

32. Buczko W. Physician utilization and expenditures in a Medicaid population. *Health Care Financing Review.* 1986;8(2):17–26.

33. Angell M. Cost containment and the physician. *Journal of the American Medical Association.* 1985;254(9):1203–1207.

34. Bodenheimer T, Fernandez A. High and rising health care costs. Part 4: Can costs be controlled while preserving quality? *Annals of Internal Medicine.* 2005;143(1):26–31.

35. Leape LL. Unnecessary surgery. *Health Services Research.* 1989; 24(3):351–407.

36. Leape LL. Unnecessary surgery. *Annual Review of Public Health.* 1992;13:363–383.

37. Ciesla G, Leader S, Stoddard J. Antibiotic prescribing rates in the US ambulatory care setting for patients diagnosed with influenza, 1997–2001. *Respiratory Medicine.* 2004;98(11):1093–1101.

38. Neilson EG, Johnson KB, Rosenbloom ST, et al. The impact of peer management on test-ordering behavior. *Annals of Internal Medicine.* 2004;141(3):196–204.

39. Feenberg D, Skinner J. Medicare transfers across states: Winners and losers. *National Tax Journal.* 2000;September:713–732.

40. Skinner J, Wennberg JE. Exceptionalism or extravagance? What's different about health care in South Florida? *Health Affairs.* 2003;(W3):W372–W375.

## Chapter 9

1. Culliton BJ. Extracting knowledge from science: A conversation with Elias Zerhouni. *Health Affairs.* 2006;25(March 9 online): w94–w103.

2. Bodeker G, Kronenberg F. A public health agenda for traditional, complementary, and alternative medicine. *American Journal of Public Health.* 2002;92(10):1582–1591.

3. Eisenberg J. *Doctors' Decisions and the Cost of Medical Care.* Ann Arbor, Michigan: Health Administration Press; 1986.

4. *Healthy People 2010: Understanding and Improving Health.* 2nd ed. Washington, DC: U.S. Government Printing Office; 2000.

5. Funk W. *Word Origins and their Romantic Stories.* New York: Bell Publishing Company; 1978.

6. Fries JF, Koop CE, Sokolov J, Beadle CE, Wright D. Beyond health promotion: Reducing the need and demand for medical care. *Health Affairs.* 1998;17(2):70–84.

7. Porter ME, Teisberg EO. Redefining competition in health care. *Harvard Business Review.* 2004;June:65–76.

8. *Towards High-Performing Health Systems.* Paris, France: Organisation for Economic Co-operation and Development; 2004.

9. Feldstein M. Health and Taxes. *Wall Street Journal.* Jan. 19, 2004: A13.

10. Forget EL, Deber R, Roos LL. Medical savings accounts: Will they reduce costs? *Canadian Medical Association Journal.* 2002;167(2): 143–147.

11. Anstadt GW. Contracting for occupational health service. An insider's view. *Journal of Occupational Medicine.* 1994;36(4):443–446.

12. Fuhrmans V. One Cure for High Health Costs: In-House Clinics at Companies. *Wall Street Journal.* Feb. 11, 2005: A1, A8.

13. Plotnikoff GA. Food as medicine—cost-effective health care? The example of omega-3 fatty acids. *Minnesota Medicine.* 2003;86(11): 41–45.

14. DeLorgeril M, Salen P, Martin JL, et al. Effects of a Mediterranean type of diet on the rate of cardiovascular complications in patients with coronary artery disease. Insights into the cardioprotective effect of certain nutriments. *Journal of the American College of Cardiology.* 1996; 28(5):1103–1108.

15. Gartside PS, Glueck CJ. The important role of modifiable dietary and behavioral characteristics in the causation and prevention of coronary heart disease hospitalization and mortality: The prospective NHANES I follow-up study. *Journal of the American College of Nutrition.* 1995;14(1):71–79.

16. Steinmetz KA, Potter JD. Vegetables, fruit, and cancer prevention: A review. *Journal of the American Dietetic Association.* 1996;96(10): 1027–1039.

17. Kohlmeier L, Simonsen N, Mottus K. Dietary modifiers of carcinogenesis. *Environmental Health Perspectives.* 1995;103(Supplement 8):177–184.

18. McCarty MF. Does a vegan diet reduce risk for Parkinson's disease? *Medical Hypotheses.* 2001;57(3):318–323.

19. Campbell JD. Lifestyle, minerals and health. *Medical Hypotheses.* 2001;57(5):521–531.

20. Willet WC. Diet, nutrition, and avoidable cancer. *Environmental Health Perspectives.* 1995;103(Supplement 8):165–170.

21. Franco OH, Bonneux L, deLaet C, Peeters A, Steyerberg EW, Mackenbach. The Polymeal: A more natural, safer, and probably tastier (than Polypill) strategy to reduce cardiovascular disease by more than 75%. *British Medical Journal.* 2004;329:1447–1459.

22. Knoops KTB, deGroot LCPGM, Kromhout D, et al. Mediterranean diet, lifestyle factors, and 10-year mortality in elderly European men and women. *Journal of the American Medical Association.* 2004;292:1433–1439.

23. Esposito K, Marfella R, Ciotola M, et al. Effect of Mediterranean-style diet on endothelial dysfunction and markers of vascular inflammation in the metabolic syndrome. *Journal of the American Medical Association.* 2004;292:1440–1446.

24. Schecter A, Li L. Dioxins, dibenzofurnas, dioxin–like PCBs, and DDE in U.S. fast food, 1995. *Chemosphere.* 1997;34(5-7):1449–1457.

25. Schecter A, Cramer P, Boggess K, Stanley J, Olson JR. Levels of dioxins, dibenzofurnas, PCB and DDE congeners in pooled food samples collected in 1995 at supermarkets across the United States. *Chemosphere.* 1997;34(5-7):1437–1447.

26. Schecter A, Dellarco M, Papke O, Olson J. A comparison of dioxins, dibenzofurans and coplanar PCBs in uncooked and broiled ground beef, catfish and bacon. *Chemosphere.* 1998;37(9-12):1723–1730.

27. Franklin BA, Khan JK. Delayed progression or regression of coronary atherosclerosis with intensive risk factor modification. Effects of diet, drugs, and exercise. *Sports Medicine.* 1996;22(5):306–320.

28. Blair SN, Horton E, Leon AS, et al. Physical activity, nutrition, and chronic disease. *Medicine and Science in Sports and Exercise.* 1995;28(3):335–349.

29. Aldana SG. Financial impact of health promotion programs: A comprehensive review of the literature. *American Journal of Health Promotion.* 2001;15(5):296–320.

30. Weed LL, Weed L. Reengineering medicine. *Federation Bulletin.* 1994;81(3):149–183.

31. Marks A. The steps still to be taken in reducing medical errors. *Christian Science Monitor.* Nov. 26, 2004. Available at: http://www.csmonitor.com/2004/1126/p02s02–uspo.html. Accessed Nov. 26, 2004.

32. Ernst FR, Grizzle AJ. Drug-related morbidity and mortality: Updating the cost-of-illness model. *Journal of the American Pharmaceutical Association.* 2001;41(2):192–199.

33. Deyo RA, Patrick DL. *Hope or Hype: The Obsession with Medical Advances and the High Cost of False Promises.* New York: AMACOM; 2005.